Diana Strickland.

They Can Make Music

Frontispiece
Ann playing the Tom-tom with a powered drumstick.

They Can Make Music

PHILIP BAILEY

With a Preface by
LADY HAMILTON

LONDON
OXFORD UNIVERSITY PRESS
NEW YORK TORONTO
1973

Oxford University Press, Ely House, London W. 1
GLASGOW NEW YORK TORONTO MELBOURNE WELLINGTON
CAPE TOWN IBADAN NAIROBI DAR ES SALAAM LUSAKA ADDIS ABABA
DELHI BOMBAY CALCUTTA MADRAS KARACHI LAHORE DACCA
KUALA LUMPUR SINGAPORE HONG KONG TOKYO

ISBN 0 19 311913 7

© Oxford University Press, 1973

All rights reserved. No part of this publication may be reproduced, stored in a retrieval system, or transmitted, in any form or by any means, electronic, mechanical, photocopying, recording, or otherwise, without the prior permission of Oxford University Press

Printed in Great Britain by
Western Printing Services Ltd,
Bristol

Preface

By Lady Hamilton,
*Chairman of the Music Panel,
the Disabled Living Foundation*

It is sad that handicapped children have at present less access to music than able-bodied children. There are many practical reasons for this situation. Handicapped children are not a large proportion of the total population of children. Those in special education, no matter what their disability, are generally in small schools with largely non-specialist staffs. Trained musicians in the field are few. The techniques of teaching mentally handicapped children are only now being researched and developed, and very little is generally known about teaching them music. With severely physically handicapped children there may be many practical difficulties to overcome before the child can make music for himself.

With such problems it is not surprising that head teachers with little knowledge of music themselves and no specialist staff may feel unable to give music its proper place in the school curriculum. Helpful information is needed to give teaching staff guidelines on how to tackle the problems of presenting music to the children in a way which will both arouse and hold their interest, and also be within their mental and physical grasp.

Mr. Bailey, with many years of pioneering and of practical experience behind him, has set out here to fill this need. He suggests simple lines of approach for the teacher in special education, who is not a musician, which are equally helpful to the musician who is not trained to teach handicapped children. He advises on the adaptations and methods which can help both the mentally handicapped child and the physically handicapped child to take part. The book is full of helpful practical information presented with unfailing humanity and unfailing common sense.

I commend this book to all those concerned with helping handicapped children other than the severely deaf. It may be that music can mean more to these children than to children without handicaps since it can be enjoyed both by those who can only advance a very small way in knowledge, or those whose bodies are so damaged that many ordinary activities are denied them.

W.M.H.

Foreword

I have frequently been asked to write a book about my work with handicapped children. Thanks to the generosity of the Carnegie United Kingdom Trust, I have now recorded some of my experiences and methods in the hope that many ideas contained in this book will prove useful to the inexperienced teacher and will assist her in the task of devising a course of instruction suitable for the young people in her charge. I should like to express my sincere thanks to the Carnegie Trust and to all those who assisted in the production of this book.

Contents

Preface	v
Foreword	vii
Introduction	xi
1 What music can do	1
2 Teaching the children	13
3 Singing	22
4 Notation	34
5 Instrumental music	47
6 Other musical activities	61
Appendices	
A Gadgets	71
B An experiment in a Special Care Unit	89
C Learning games	94
List of recommended music	122
Bibliography	138
Useful addresses	143

*This book is respectfully dedicated to
the Convener of the Arts Committee
of the Carnegie United Kingdom Trust,
The Right Hon. The Countess of Albemarle.*

Introduction

Very many years' experience of music making with handicapped children suffering from a variety of disabilities has convinced me that the medical, psychological, and social benefits to the child far outweigh its musical value. Success in music making often sparks off the desire to attempt other activities.

I do not wish to give the impression that music will always be successful in helping the handicapped child to overcome his disability, but I have no hesitation in saying that in a large number of cases, given a suitably trained teacher who has infinite patience and the ability to adapt his methods to suit the capacity and handicap of the individual child, many things considered impossible a few years ago can now be accomplished. I assume that anyone undertaking this type of work is not only a lover of children, but also has a genuine desire to help the handicapped child. If you consider this work is 'just a job', then this profession is not for you. I would stress the fact that, if it is at all possible to arouse and help the children, one of the best introductions to many new, interesting, and beneficial experiences is music.

When writing this volume, I have assumed that the majority of my readers will be either students or teachers who have had very little experience with physically or mentally handicapped children, and may not only include teachers who work in special care units or hospital schools, but also people who, although not teachers, are responsible for the care of some of these youngsters. Therefore, I have included some information and advice which will be superfluous in the case of the experienced teacher.

Normal healthy Infants and Juniors could definitely benefit from some of the methods outlined in the following chapters, which would enable them to participate in a much greater

Introduction

variety of musical activities, and at a considerably earlier age, than is possible if orthodox methods of teaching are used.

With so many grades and varieties of handicap, it is impossible to provide a ready-made solution to all the teacher's problems. But the ideas contained in this book may serve as a guide and may possibly inspire those in charge of the children to modify some of my methods to conform with their own special problems. All the suggestions made in this volume are the result of long experience and observation of many forms of handicap, and do not necessarily apply only to the teaching of music. It has been proved that in many cases where apathy previously prevailed, the first successful method of evoking a response from the children was through music and musical activities.

I would urge you to remember that every success the handicapped child has brings him one step nearer to the achievements of the able-bodied youngster, and this is one of our most important tasks. Music is one of the keys which will unlock many doors, and successful participation in very simple musical activities has often resulted in gradual progress in other directions.

1 What music can do

There are still some parents of disabled children who consider that the child is so very handicapped that he must be treated as a baby and never taught even to attempt to do very simple things for himself. This is one of the greatest mistakes to make. Always assist the child to help himself as much as possible within the limits imposed by his handicap. If necessary, provide him with any gadgets that will enable him to perform simple tasks. Most physically fit people use some kind of aids, such as the bath back-brush, spectacles, opera glasses, dentures, cosmetics, or a magnifying glass.

A young boy who has a leg disability told me that when he was at school his mother said to him: 'The fact that your legs will not allow you to run as fast as the other boys does not mean that your brain will not allow you to be top of your form, providing you study carefully.' This boy was fortunate in having a very wise mother who encouraged her child to endeavour to make progress in every way possible. Others are not so lucky.

Some people appear to be under the impression that anyone confined to a wheelchair is a different creature and should not be treated as an ordinary person, notwithstanding the fact that in a high percentage of cases the disabled occupant of a wheelchair has a perfectly normal brain. The following examples will illustrate my point:

In the first case, two girls in their late twenties were pushing in a wheelchair another girl of approximately the same age. She was quite normal apart from the fact that she was unable to walk. They met a lady who was apparently an acquaintance of one of the girls. She greeted her friend and then said:

'Miss Perkins, may I introduce my friend Miss Thorpe?' Miss Perkins shook hands and said: 'Delighted to meet you, Miss Thorpe.' But when the girl introduced her handicapped friend she merely said: 'This is Jean,' and Miss Perkins, without offering to shake hands, cheerfully said: 'Hello, Jean,' thus giving the impression that, because Jean was unable to use her legs, she was some kind of inferior creature to be treated as a child.

On another occasion, when I was taking a Music Group at a holiday course arranged for members of one of the P.H.A.B. clubs (these are youth clubs for both physically handicapped and ablebodied young folk, hence the 'PHAB' title) a man about twenty-five years of age, who was quite normal mentally and had full use of his hands and arms, asked me: 'Why is it impossible for a person in a wheelchair to play a guitar?' I said: 'Of course you can learn to play a guitar'; he replied: 'I don't want to become a marvellous performer, but I thought it would be nice if I could learn to strum a few chords, and then we could sometimes have a sing-song in the evenings; but at the residential home for handicapped persons where I live I am always told that anyone in a wheelchair cannot play a guitar.' This type of treatment, if continued, cannot fail to give the handicapped person an inferiority complex, and in many cases may make him afraid to attempt anything that appears at all difficult. Obviously a person with severe brain damage in addition to a physical disability may only be able to acquire a few very simple skills, but, however badly damaged a person is, he should be assisted to do anything within his capacity.

When organizing any musical activity I always include every child if I can possibly devise any method which will enable the youngster to overcome his special difficulties. I will use the most unorthodox methods imaginable, rather than fail to help the child. Some people may say I cheat; perhaps they are right. I certainly have no conscience when helping the handicapped child. My usual method is to include them by fair means if possible, but to use foul means if other methods fail. Some of the children's problems at first seem almost insurmountable, but I usually manage to find a solution.

There was, for instance, a severely subnormal girl who could play a series of chime bars with a reasonable degree of accuracy if the notes she had to play were of one beat's duration; but I tried every conceivable method of explaining and demonstrating the duration of a two beat note, without any success whatever. After considering the problem for a time, I decided that, as fair means had not been successful, I must 'cheat' rather than omit the girl from the concert for which we were preparing. I finally overcame the difficulty by arranging the chime bars close together for the one beat notes, and leaving a good space after the two beat notes, thus: 111112 . . . . 1111112 . . . . 1111 etc. As you will observe, since a space was left after the two beat note, she was unable to reach and play the following note until a period of two beats had elapsed.

On the night of the concert, before the performance commenced, the chime bars were arranged on a small table with the notes all correctly spaced. When she played her item the timing was perfect. The fact that she had been able to join the other members of her group in playing this item certainly raised her morale, and when I looked at the happy child I was firmly convinced that my action in 'cheating' was fully justified.

(In the course of this book I shall suggest various ways in which the instruments, the music, or both, can be adapted to enable even seriously handicapped children, whether mentally or physically, to participate in musical activities.)

Many years ago, when I was discussing with my own doctor the needs of handicapped children, he remarked: 'Almost anything within reason that will add to the happiness and confidence of the patient cannot fail to be beneficial.' My own experiences confirm the truth of this statement, as I have certainly found that in many cases a sense of achievement, obtained through success in very simple music making, has sparked off within the child a desire to explore the possibility of success in other activities. There is no doubt that we cannot overestimate the psychological value of the sense of achievement the child feels when he does succeed—often after a hard struggle—in performing some simple task.

Here is a typical example of a case I had in a unit for very severely subnormal children. A ten-year-old boy named John defied all attempts on the part of the staff to induce him to taken an interest in anything. He could not be taught to attend to his own needs or to feed himself. He sat still, apparently oblivious to anything happening in the room. One day, after many weeks of music making with a group of the other children, he got up and, picking up the hammer, struck a chime bar once only. When he showed interest in the chime bar, I devoted a considerable amount of time in an attempt to induce him to play other notes, but he was only interested in the one chime bar. Every time I pointed to 'his' chime bar he struck the note.

About this time I was rehearsing some members of the group in preparation for a concert in which I combined able-bodied children with children suffering from a variety of disabilities, so I decided to include a special part for one chime bar. He was brought to the rehearsals in the concert hall and placed right in front of the instrumental group opposite the Conductor. In order that the members of the audience should not realize that he could only play one note, I arranged a full set of chime bars on the table in front of him, with a good space between the note he played and the remainder of the notes. As an additional precaution I stuck a strip of red paper on 'his' note. This worked perfectly. On the night of the concert John duly took his place behind the table and carefully struck the note when the conductor pointed to it with his baton. I do not think that anyone in the audience realized that he struck the same note every time.

The hall was packed and the item received great applause. John apparently realized that for the first time in his life he had participated in an important event. He had never spoken to us previously but, in spite of his seeming indifference to events happening in the unit, he had obviously listened to the other children and members of the staff talking and could himself speak, because he started saying to almost everyone with whom he came in contact: 'I'm in the Band! I'm in the Band!'

Having discovered that he could do something important gave him confidence and aroused the desire to attempt other activities. His next success occurred a few days later when, a member of staff having removed his shoes, he immediately attempted to put on his slippers and, after a struggle, succeeded. His next venture was to wander into the kitchen, pick up a handful of cutlery and carry it into the dining-room, where he placed the articles in a heap on the table. Although he could not set them out in the correct order, he was encouraged to help set the table and he very gradually extended the scope of his activities. His progress was extremely slow, but he did acquire a number of simple skills. This success was undoubtedly due to his initial effort with the chime bar.

Della was another girl to whom music had a psychological value. On one occasion after taking a music class consisting of mentally sick teenage girls, I was asked if I would interview a new patient who was only interested in music. I was informed that it was essential that we should be alone when I interviewed her, as she was exceedingly jealous and immediately became very violent unless she received all the attention. I agreed to see the girl, and Della was brought into the room by one of the staff and we were introduced. She was a pretty girl, fifteen years of age, very polite, and apparently a nice girl. An inexperienced person would have wondered why she

They Can Make Music

was in the unit, as she appeared quite normal. I had been told that she had not shown any sign of mental abnormality until she was thirteen years of age, and that she had then suddenly changed. She had always been very musical and had been taking lessons from a lady who was an experienced teacher of music. The girl's progress had been excellent until she started to display a violent temper if anyone refused to accede to her requests. On several occasions she caused scenes when her teacher refused to extend her music period as she had another student waiting. After several incidents of this type the teacher discontinued her music lessons. Although she had medical attention her condition became worse and she was sent to the mental unit for treatment. I spoke to her about her music and she answered quite normally. After a few minutes' conversation I asked her to play one of her favourite pieces; her performance was extremely good and there was no doubt about her musicianship. She would, under different circumstances, almost certainly have obtained a music studentship and could have made music her career. I usually spent about half an hour helping her each time I visited the unit. All appeared to be progressing satisfactorily. I was told that she enjoyed her music and that whenever she showed any sign of becoming violent a suggestion that she should go and practise her music, as I would soon be coming to hear her play, usually calmed her down and she immediately went to the piano. After a few weeks I was warned that she was really getting to like me, because I helped her with the music, which was her one remaining pleasure. The difficulty was that when she had one of her violent turns she always attempted to strangle the people she liked; she simply ignored those she disliked. I was not really worried, because I was certain that she would devote all her attention to the music. I never had the slightest trouble with her; she always thanked me for her lesson and never failed to apologize if she made a mistake when playing. She really made progress and I was informed that the music was having a stabilizing effect upon her mentality. She eventually improved considerably, was transferred to a unit near her home, and was eventually discharged as cured.

Vincent, a subnormal child aged 9, belongs to a musical family and was brought to me for advice. I arranged for him to receive instruction from a very understanding teacher who, acting on my advice, taught him to play extremely simple parts in items being performed by some of her normal students. This has given him a sense of achievement and also a considerable amount of pleasure. His parents report a great improvement in his general behaviour.

Elaine was a backward child, aged 10. Although classed as very backward, she was really suffering from an inferiority complex, caused by being overshadowed by her clever brothers and sisters; she was considered the stupid member of the family. Fortunately a friend of her parents persuaded her mother to come to me for advice, as he had noticed that Elaine appeared to listen to music. After interviewing first the mother and later both mother and child, I decided that music, if properly presented, could aid in the development of this girl. Her parents agreed to allow her to have music lessons, if I would recommend a suitable teacher. This I was able to do, and Elaine is gradually gaining more confidence, not only in her ability to make music, but in many other ways.

Olga is a mentally handicapped girl aged 15. Her parents noticed that she appeared to listen with interest to many different kinds of music. They consulted me and, although she is too low grade to attempt anything except very elementary music, she is now receiving training suitable for a girl with a very low I.Q., and is happily making slow progress and appears to be gaining more confidence.

Ronnie was a nice little mentally handicapped four-year-old; his response to music was unique in my experience. As soon as he heard music of any kind he immediately went under the nearest table, undressed completely, and sat listening quite intently, and apparently with great pleasure, to the sound of the music. As soon as the music ceased he dressed himself and emerged from under the table. We could not persuade him to play an instrument or to join in the singing, but he was certainly a keen listener.

Music is equally useful in helping the physically handicapped child. I recall a girl named Joan who, for the first six years of her life, was unable to walk. When she was six-and-a-half, she had an operation which gave her partial use of her legs, but when she returned to the unit she was afraid to attempt to walk and especially afraid to bend her knees. Before her operation I had been teaching her, and other children, music by means of an elaborate colour scheme I had devised for those with severe brain injuries in addition to physical handicaps.

This, very briefly, included matched frocks, toys, instruments, etc. Joan was a 'green' child in this colour scheme and one morning, when some of the other children were playing football with various coloured balls, a green ball accidentally rolled to her feet. She looked down at the ball and, noticing it was green, instinctively kicked it away without realizing that she had bent her knee. I then arranged for the ball to keep rolling in her direction and each time she responded to the colour urge and kicked it away, so we decided to include her in the football group. At first we let her remain seated, but later induced her to stand up supported by two attendants. The next stage was to stop the ball a short distance away and she then attempted, slowly but successfully, to step forward in order to kick the ball. This was the start of her real attempts at walking, and within a few weeks she could walk, first with the assistance of a member of the staff and later supporting herself with a walking aid, and finally walking slowly but surely completely unaided. This result was certainly due to her interest in learning music, as the association between her music colour and the matching colour of the football induced her to move her leg spontaneously when the ball approached her.

Diane is an eight-year-old child who holds her hands with the palms facing each other in a 'clap hands' position. If she wishes to lift a cup to her mouth, she presses the palms of her hands on the sides of the cup and, thus holding it, moves the cup to her mouth. She is interested in music and expressed a desire to play a small electric organ which is in her home. This she attempted to play by holding her hands with the palms facing each other and producing the sounds with a 'chopping' motion.

When I examined her fingers I discovered that, although her digitals were as weak as those of a six-month-old child, she could, with some assistance from me, turn her wrists until the palms of her hands faced the keyboard, and I was also able to help her to make a very small movement with each finger. The thumbs on both hands were missing. After a few hours' practice, and with a considerable amount of guidance and assistance from me, she found—to her great delight—that, although she still experienced a considerable amount of difficulty, she could touch the keys of the organ and produce sounds by moving her digitals individually. Her parents were very surprised and delighted at her achievement. Apparently she had never previously attempted to move her fingers individually and her parents had assumed that she was unable to do so. She also has difficulty with both her elbow and wrist joints. Her legs, however, are absolutely normal.

She is now receiving music lessons from a teacher who is skilled in instructing the disabled, and she can now very slowly play the organ using both hands simultaneously. Her brain is normal and she is learning to read musical notation. She derives much pleasure from her newly-found ability to make music. This achievement has also had considerable psychological value in addition to its undoubted therapeutic importance. Her success has added to her happiness and confidence, and her successful efforts to depress the keys of the organ will gradually increase the strength and flexibility of her fingers, thus enabling her to attempt many things that were impossible a few months ago. (She can now depress the much heavier piano keys.)

The use of music and special gadgets can, in suitable cases, make the child enjoy participation in therapy sessions and will not only help to accelerate the restoration of flexibility and strength to the child's limbs, but also make the task of the therapist easier, as she will usually secure the maximum amount of co-operation from the young patients. When we induce the individual on the learning end of the treatment to anticipate with pleasure the performance of the various essential movements, progress is almost certain to be speeded up.

One gadget which will help to induce a small child to practise wrist rotation exercises consists of a musical box. This will only play when the child turns the handle; when the tune ends, up pops a 'Jack-in-the-Box'. The child has a toy to play with and does not realize that he is performing a wrist rotation exercise every time he turns the handle. An adjustment to the gears will compel the child to make a much larger rotary movement if necessary.

The double-headed drumstick is also an excellent exercise for forearm rotation. If used in conjunction with records requiring drum rolls at intervals the young patient almost invariably enjoys the music session.

To induce finger movement when a child has his hand or arm in plaster, finger puppets have proved quite effective. Foot puppets and occasionally toe puppets are also useful; a good supply of these puppets in various sizes is essential, as different types of puppet must be used if the interest of the patient is to be maintained.

For the child who has to lie on his back and exercise his legs by raising and lowering them a number of times, the monotony of this action will be relieved if the leg movements are synchronized with the music of suitable lively records. If the records are changed at fairly frequent intervals, or a tape containing a number of appropriate tunes is used, the interest of the patient will be retained.

On some occasions it is possible to have a small group of children, each playing an instrument that will induce the child to make the movements necessary to help to cure his defects.

The use of an electronic organ has been found of great value in helping young people gradually to regain strength and flexibility in their fingers.

Sometimes it is almost impossible to separate music teaching from music therapy. For example, a girl who had weak fingers on her left hand discovered that she could not press the strings of a cello, which she was anxious to play. The simple solution was to re-string her instrument, reverse the bridge, and change the position of the sound post. Thus she used the strong fingers of her right hand to stop the strings and the weak arm for bowing. As a result she was able to receive music lessons and later joined the school orchestra. After a few months she found that the bowing of her instrument had strengthened her weak arm. Thus, education and therapy are combined. Another example of how music can have a psychological as well as an educational value was the results obtained with a boy with only one finger on one hand and two fingers on the other hand. He was most anxious to play a trumpet. The provision of a special stand to hold the instrument has solved his problem. He is now receiving tuition and will later become a member of a brass band.

At the present time the author is engaged on developing further aids for those suffering from disabilities. The list of therapeutic aids already developed (on p. 71) will, it is hoped, suggest to the therapist other ways of utilizing music to help the patient to achieve better results.

There is no valid reason why a really musical child should not be trained to become a professional musician. Teachers of music who are confined to wheelchairs can equal their physically fit colleagues in efficiency. Their only real disadvantage lies in the fact that lack of easy access in some buildings may restrict their movements. This difficulty will be gradually overcome as authorities improve means of approach. In the schools for physically handicapped children a partially handicapped teacher is a definite asset to the youngsters, as their teacher, having suffered from a disability herself, will, as a result of her own experiences, be in a position to give the maximum amount of assistance to the children in coping with their difficulties. Furthermore, the fact that a person as badly disabled as themselves has managed to overcome her disability, to the extent of achieving such an important position as a teacher, cannot fail to arouse within some of the pupils the feeling that they also could occupy important positions, if they really work and study carefully.

Music making, if carefully selected to accord with the capabilities of the disabled person, is often one of the skills which the handicapped individual can acquire and which will not only give pleasure to the performers but also to those listening to the music. It is also a very useful and fruitful group activity, as those participating can be taught instruments selected to give maximum results with the minimum of effort on the part of the badly handicapped person, and the combination of those only able to play elementary music with others who can acquire greater skills produces a pleasing ensemble that not only sounds quite impressive to the listeners, but also has great psychological value in adding to the confidence of the musicians.

2 Teaching the children

When attempting to teach handicapped children, one of your first thoughts should be: 'How can I assist this child to achieve some of the things the able-bodied youngster can accomplish?' and always remember that, in the case of the very severely handicapped child, a sub-standard result is a real achievement, and that you are not taking a class of twenty youngsters, but twenty individuals, many of whom will require a different approach from that suitable for their fellow members. As far as possible treat them as you would able-bodied children; do not give the impression that you consider them different from other people.

One of the first things to be taught is a reasonable amount of discipline; without this the children will not make progress. Owing to the variety of handicaps, and the fact that you may sometimes find a considerable age range within a single group, it is impossible to make any rules that will be suitable for every occasion. Much has to be left to the discretion of the teacher, who has the responsibility of deciding how to cope with the various situations as they arise. This is a much more difficult proposition than when dealing with ordinary children, as so many factors have to be taken into account. When correcting adolescents, stress the fact that they are now almost 'grown-ups' and should behave accordingly, and not act like naughty children. I have found this method quite effective.

The teacher must, however, always remember that the handicapped child, whether suffering from a mental or physical defect, is often extremely acute in discovering ways of avoiding anything he does not wish to do, and is equally ingenious in devising methods for getting his own way. An example of this occurred at one of the places I visited. An extremely fat teenage girl had, for some reason we never discovered, a great objection to washing her hands. As soon as the youngsters were told to go and wash their hands this girl immediately threw herself on the floor, knowing that no member of the staff could lift her single-handed; the result invariably was that another member of staff had to be called to assist in getting the girl on her feet again. This continued for some time until a new member of staff was appointed. The new lady was a strong young woman, and had no difficulty in lifting the girl single-handed. After this had happened a few times the girl ceased to throw herself on the floor if the new member of staff was about, but always reverted to her old habit if any other member of staff was on duty.

Just like any others, handicapped children will almost invariably 'try out' the new teacher to discover if they can misbehave without bringing trouble upon themselves; but if the children are handled carefully from the start they will not be too bad. Always be kind and friendly, but very firm. Be scrupulously fair in your dealings with the children, and always keep any promises you may make. Once they understand that when you say 'no' you really mean 'no', you will soon have them under control. The more successful you are in disciplining a child and arousing confidence in his own ability—and in yours—the easier your task will become. In addition, you are helping the child to become a happier, more self-reliant person.

To get the very best results from the child, you must be a master of the art of improvisation and informal presentation, and the utmost care must be taken in the preparation of the lessons, so do not fail to 'do your homework' very thoroughly.

When assessing the possibilities of making music with the physically handicapped child, you should carefully observe his movements. Can he move his arms, hands, fingers, legs, feet, head? Is he able to move his arms outwards and inwards, up and down, and to what extent? This information will enable you to select the most suitable instrument for each child or to decide if the instrument will require some modification, or possibly a supporting stand. Unlike the able-bodied youngster, the physically handicapped child must not only learn to play the chosen instrument, but may also have to cope with the restricted movement of his limbs and the fact that they may not move at the requisite speed. Test the child with several different types of instrument before making a final decision. If he cannot use his hands, can he play an instrument using his feet, mouth, head? Are there any 'aids' available to help this youngster with his music making?

When your group consists of mentally handicapped youngsters, you should first observe their general behaviour; always explain everything in the most simple way possible, whenever the child encounters difficulties in his efforts to make music. Very many repetitions and demonstrations may be necessary before the child understands your requirements. Before scolding a child for disobeying your instructions, be absolutely certain that he really knows what you expect him to do. Orders which are crystal clear to you, and which may be understood by most of the children, could be beyond the comprehension of the particular child you are instructing at the moment. If a child has not obeyed your order to bring a certain article to you, do not immediately scold him. Re-phrase your order in the most simple language possible, using your hand to direct the child to the object you wish him to collect.

Most children who have severe mental defects can only concentrate for a very short period. Therefore, each item can only continue for a brief period. Be prepared to introduce something fresh at frequent intervals, later returning to the first subject. After something active, introduce an item requiring the quiet attention of the group; this usually produces the best results. The method I found most successful was to assemble a number of different types of simple instruments, and allow a small group of children to spend about five minutes learning to play a very easy tune. We would spend the next five minutes playing with balloons. At the end of the period we resumed the music lesson, but this time we played the same tune on xylophones. These I made especially for this group. They consisted of small stands, each supporting a single note. Therefore, they could be used singly or collectively as required. Every five minutes we changed from music to games, returning again and again to the music lesson. We always played the same tune but each time we used a different instrument: single note dulcimers which I also constructed, slians (tuned nails), pitch pipes, and other simple single-note melodic instruments. The fact that they spent all the music period on learning the same tune did not matter; by changing the instruments after each game, the novelty of producing musical sounds in a different way each time retained their interest throughout the entire period. I always planned a lesson period of fifty minutes. Twenty minutes of this period was for teaching music, twenty minutes for games and the remainder I allowed for the time spent in changing over.

Both the mentally and the physically handicapped children are often subject to fluctuations in health from day to day, and this sometimes affects their general behaviour. This important fact should not be forgotten when dealing with these children. In your approach to the individual child you must always consider his mental and physical condition at the moment when you are instructing him. Unless your methods are 'tailor-made' to fit the child's mentality, you cannot get the best response from him.

It is very important that you should know as much as possible about all the children in your care: their handicaps, mental age and medical history. This information will enable you to obtain better results when you are teaching them. Always work in full co-operation with the medical and other members of the staff. Before taking charge of a new group ask if there is anything special you should know about the children.

The person in charge is usually very willing to help you. If a child's case history is available, study it carefully. It may prevent you from taking action that could possibly be harmful to the child. I know of one teacher who was in charge of a group of physically handicapped youngsters, many of whom were of a rather low grade mentally. One boy had a much higher I.Q. than the majority of the class. He was also very obedient and reliable. When the teacher required anything that was in another part of the building, Ronnie was always chosen as the messenger. The teacher had been with her class for six months, before she accidentally discovered that Ronnie suffered from a heart defect and was supposed to avoid exertion and to rest as much as possible. All the other members of the staff already had this information and assumed that the new teacher was also aware of the nature of his disability. Never fail to research into the history of every individual who may join your class at a later date.

When teaching a child with a mental age of two years, very gradually introduce methods and tasks suitable for a child about three to six months older. It is important to ensure that, if it is at all possible, every child should participate in all the activities. Never omit one child, as this would certainly add to the already considerable inferiority complex from which many handicapped children suffer. One good way to help to build up a child's morale is to try and find some special little job for as many children as possible. This is especially important when dealing with the very low grade child. Even a really backward child will usually feel important if, for example, you ask her to collect a music book from the table and bring it to you. Even though at first she may not quite understand and fail to carry out your instructions correctly, give her some encouragement and let her make another attempt. At least she is trying—sometimes very 'trying', but she is not to blame, so be patient! Never fail to praise children when they perform any task correctly. Allow some of the mobile children to take turns in distributing the instruments and use other children to collect them and bring them to you when the lesson period is completed.

If you have a mixture of physically handicapped children and educationally subnormal youngsters, some of the physically fit, though subnormal, children can be trained to help physically handicapped children up or down steps, and could also push wheelchairs if necessary. Sometimes it is possible to ask a few of the children, who are making reasonable progress with their music, to help by acting as 'tutors' to other, less gifted members. They could be given very simple tasks—such as showing a child how to manipulate a simple instrument. Older children enjoy playing 'teacher' and will normally be delighted to co-operate. If you have a bedfast child who shows any signs of intelligence, make this youngster one of your priorities for a job of some kind. The child who is unable to leave her bed gets a tremendous thrill if you bring one or two small children to her bedside and ask her to help you by showing the children how to overcome some small difficulty they have encountered in the music.

At one of the places previously known as Junior Training Centres, I was usually met by several children, each anxious to carry my music case. In order to prevent any disappointment, I invariably opened my case and gave each child some music to carry to the piano. At another place I am met by a senior mentally handicapped child, who has been trained to help with the younger children. He removes my hat and coat, carefully places them on the stand and then escorts me to the music teacher. When I leave he assists me with my coat, buttons it and puts my hat on my head, often at a rather unusual angle. Allowing the children to perform simple tasks helps in their development.

Many of the children will have considerable problems of one kind and another, and overcoming them will tax both your patience and your ingenuity. But do not give up; I have found that hardly any child is completely untouched by music, even those who at first appear to be unable to respond in any way.

Roger, a five-year-old autistic child who attended a special care unit, spent most of his time sitting in a corner apparently oblivious of everything. The only time he displayed any interest was when he noticed I was approaching the piano. He would leave his corner, go to the toy cupboard and collect a scooter, place one foot upon it and wait for the music to commence. As soon as I started to play, he would travel around the room, increasing or decreasing his speed as the tempo of the music changed. If the music ceased he came to an abrupt halt and looked towards the piano. If I was changing the music, he waited, resuming his travels as soon as he heard the sound of a new melody. But when I removed the music and walked away he dropped the scooter and returned to his corner. We were unable to persuade him to play any instrument, but he evidently enjoyed the sound of music and this was his method of participating. At a much later stage he occasionally joined in a few simple activities.

Percy, aged four, was another autistic child who apparently felt the need for isolation. He would crawl under a large rug or remove a bed-spread from one of the cots, and cover himself completely. On other occasions he would arrange a number of chairs in a circle with himself in the centre. When the other children played their percussion instruments, he would very slowly open the cover in which he was wrapped until his entire face was visible. He apparently enjoyed listening to the music and after a period of about three months he was persuaded to join the band. From this time onwards he very gradually responded to other stimulants, but after about twelve months he was transferred to another area, where I hope he continued his very slow development.

Sandra was a pretty little eight-year-old child. I met her when visiting a school for very low grade children. The teacher in charge of Sandra's group told me that the children were only able to play by rote extremely simple percussion music, and that melodic percussion was quite beyond their capabilities. 'They all attempt to play, although they make many mistakes. I said all', she continued, 'but I should have said, all except one child; Sandra is her name. She is a complete write-off and cannot be persuaded to join the others. When they play, she just doodles in her copy-book.'

I watched Sandra very closely during the music period and noticed that when the music was soft she made small circles on the paper. These circles gradually became larger as the volume of the music increased, and were reduced in size when the music became softer. Her pencil also moved faster or slower as the tempo of the music varied. When I drew the teacher's attention to Sandra's reaction to the music, she was amazed and said that, although Sandra had been in her group for two years, she had not noticed that the child was really paying close attention to both the tempo and volume of the music.

Moral: Study all the children in your charge very carefully, before you decide that anyone is a write-off.

Any success the child may have will also add to the happiness of the parents when they observe that their youngster is making some progress, however slow this may be. Every time the child can participate in a concert or other event this boosts the morale of both the child and the parents.

It is infinitely worth while finding a way in which music can reach all the children in your care, and encouraging it for the good it does them, psychologically as well as physically.

A few words to those who may be about to commence teaching in a hospital school: conditions will, naturally, vary in different hospitals; the teacher may find some children in the wards are grouped according to age, others according to disability, but most grouped according to medical needs. They could include those physically or mentally handicapped and the ages could range from the pre-school child to the adolescent.

Long wards add to the difficulty of obtaining a focal point for the music group. If possible, have the beds moved closer and place your mobile patients in the centre or between beds. If you can play a guitar or autoharp, use it in preference to the piano, which is sometimes in a worse condition than some of the patients. A small electronic organ or a minipiano is quite useful. The autoharp and chordal dulcimer can be used, together with other tuned and untuned percussion. Foot, finger, hand, and arm puppets not only entertain the children, but provide useful exercise. Use as many children as possible.

If you have a co-operative Ward Sister (and they are in the majority) you can do much useful work. You will find both long stay and those who are only in for a short period. In one hospital I visited recently the patients included a teenage boy whose leg had been injured in a car accident. The teacher was helping him with preparation for his 'O' levels.

In the hospital school itself you are subject to interruptions when patients are removed for medical and nursing requirements such as physiotherapy and other forms of treatment. The unexpected arrival of one of the consultants could result in a child having to suspend his lesson. In hospitals where parents are permitted to visit at almost any time, the arrival of Elsie's Mum could also be a reason for her removal from your music group.

Although there are some disadvantages, this work is really worth the extra effort that may be necessary in order to achieve good results.

3 Singing

When introducing the handicapped child to the pleasures of making music, we must not forget that many of the children have experienced failure on other occasions; therefore it is essential that, in order to arouse and retain the child's interest in music, we must devise a system that will enable him to attain success in the shortest possible time, and with the minimum effort on the part of the child. Do not be afraid to use unorthodox methods if you consider that they will help to speed progress.

When teaching anything new to children, always try to introduce something with which they are already familiar; e.g. when teaching young children a nursery rhyme such as 'Little Miss Muffet', it is most unlikely that they will be familiar with the meaning of 'tuffet' or 'curds and whey'. Why not substitute something with which they are familiar, 'a chair' instead of 'a tuffet' and 'chips' instead of 'curds and whey'? Our revised version would read:

> Little girl Claire
> Sat on a chair
> Eating some chips one day,
> A very big spider,
> Sat down beside her,
> Little girl Claire ran away.

Or consider the suitability of using 'Little Polly Flinders' in its present form. In these days of central heating and the extensive use of gas and electric fires, many children will not understand the word 'cinders', and how many people still use the word 'whip'? Therefore, our rhyme could be revised as follows:

> Little Mary Moore,
> Sat upon the floor,
> Counting all her bare pink toes.
> Her mother came and caught her,
> And smacked her little daughter
> For spoiling all her nice new clothes.

Nearly all children are familiar with the words 'chair', 'chips' and 'floor', and almost all small children know from painful experience the meaning of the word 'smack'!

The use of a limited amount of 'pop' music is frequently of value, as most children will be famliar with this type of music, and you are almost certain to get a more rapid response from the children than would be the case if you used unfamiliar items. I do not suggest that you should confine your repertoire to 'pop', but that you should start at the level of the majority and very gradually introduce the lighter kind of standard music.

When teaching a group of children to sing, you will find that your task is made a little easier if you arrange the members of your group in the following order: in the front row place all the children who experience difficulty in singing at the correct pitch. In the second row place all your best singers, and in the third row arrange all your mediocre singers. The advantages of this arrangement will be obvious. Those who have pitch difficulties will have their teacher facing them, and in the row behind are those who can sing in tune. Therefore, the 'drones' hear correct pitch both in front and behind them and the mediocre children in the third row can only hear the good singing by the children who are immediately in front of them, and so cannot be put off pitch by the erratic singing of those in the front row. If any of the children really cannot be taught to sing in tune, and they are only a small minority, do not send them away. Give them a few chime bars and arrange for them to accompany the singers.

When the children can sing in unison with a reasonable degree of confidence, the next step is to teach them to sing

They Can Make Music

rounds in two parts. If it is possible to obtain the assistance of someone who can play any melodic instrument that is different from the one played by the teacher, the children's progress will undoubtedly be considerably accelerated. Almost any kind of instrument can be used, e.g. piano and melodica, violin and clarinet, chime bars and xylophone, harmonica and recorder. The method I have found most successful is to teach the rounds in three easy stages.

Stage one: divide the class into two equal groups and place them at opposite ends of the room. The teacher has her children grouped around the piano, or whatever instrument she can play. The person playing the second instrument has her children in similar formation. The children in each group are first given the opportunity of hearing their leader play the round on her instrument. They are then told to follow their leader and only sing the tune she plays. Then allow each group to practise separately, singing to La, until they are quite familiar with the tune. Then let the groups combine, still singing to La, the teacher's group starting and the other group joining in at the appropriate point. When both groups can accurately follow their leader, add the words. At this point you may have to revert to the original method of letting one group sing whilst the other children remain silent. Then resume singing in the normal way. Later allow group two to commence and group one to follow on; teach them a few rounds, still keeping the groups apart. When the members of both groups can sing their own part correctly and they are not affected by the singing of the children at the other end of the room, very gradually move the groups closer until each group, aided by its instrumentalist, can sing reasonably well, notwithstanding the close proximity of the other group; they are now ready to proceed to the next stage.

Stage two: return the groups to their original positions. Ask them to sing the same rounds, but this time the instrumentalist only plays the first phrase. If the children cannot continue the round unaided they will, of course, require more assistance from their leader, but keep this to the minimum. Gradually reduce the distance between the children until they merge into one group.

Stage three: return them to their initial positions. This time their leaders sing with them instead of using an instrument, gradually bringing them together again. Finally let the groups endeavour to sing without any assistance from their leaders.

Some of my readers may consider this method is rather time-consuming, but if you are dealing with children with very low I.Q.s this system will provide a fairly safe foundation upon which to build your two-part singing.

One useful aid, when teaching the children to sing in tune, is to sound a suitable note on a chime bar and let them try to sing the entire alphabet on this note. In the early stages it is advisable to strike the chime bar once for each letter of the alphabet. Let the youngsters sing slowly, taking a short breath between each letter. When they have had a considerable amount of practice and can pitch the note with a reasonable degree of accuracy play the chime bar on alternate letters. When they are capable of retaining the correct pitch throughout, very gradually reduce the amount of assistance given by the chime bar until they can sing from A to Z correctly after the teacher has only sounded the first note. It is also advisable to sound the chime bar when they reach Z as a means of enabling the children to check the accuracy of their pitch. It will almost certainly be a considerable time before they can manage without some assistance and the teacher must be ready to sound the note if there is the slightest deviation from the correct pitch.

If you always arrange the children in the order previously suggested, you will eventually succeed in getting the group to sing in tune, although 100 per cent success cannot be expected in every case. When teaching this pitch exercise, repeat several times on different notes.

Another method is to choose four children as 'Music'; place them in front of the class and sing on one note, e.g. Jean, Percy, John, Grace. Repeat using other children. If a child repeatedly sings above or below the correct pitch, ask the youngster to sing any note he wishes. When he produces a recognizable sound say: 'That is John's note. Let us all sing it.' The children all sing: 'John, John, John,' repeating the note at the pitch John has sung. Ask John to sing 'his' note again, but this time the other children sing with him. When John can pitch his note accurately, ask another child to sing a note. Then say: 'That is Fred's note. Let us all sing it with him.' The class sings: 'Fred, Fred, Fred,' John endeavouring to join in the singing. On future occasions commence the singing lesson by first asking John and the other children to sing 'his' note. This is followed by Fred singing his note, assisted by John and the remainder of the group. Later, add a third child singing his special note. In the majority of cases John gradually discovers that he can produce recognizable sounds at the correct pitch. The next step is to ask John to sing 'his' note, followed by the teacher singing a sound a little above or below the one he can produce the most successfully. If necessary play both 'his' and the new note on chime bars. The other children join in singing the two notes.

When a child has an unusual amount of difficulty in sounding a note at the correct pitch, it is sometimes possible to assist him by blowing a note on a melodica held close to his ear; if this fails, try other instruments, e.g. violin, recorder, chime bar. Some children can hear with greater clarity and, therefore, reproduce with greater ease a sound produced by a stringed instrument, than the same note obtained by blowing a wind instrument, or by hitting a xylophone with a hammer. This is especially noticeable in the case of some partially deaf children, whose hearing may be more defective in some sections of the normal aural range than in others. Therefore, a high-pitched sound could possibly be heard by one child, whereas another child could only hear the lower sounds with any degree of clarity. I have frequently noticed that some educationally subnormal and also severely subnormal children find that singing aids the memory. For example, one group of children, who were taught to recite some simple rhymes and very short verses of poetry, had almost completely forgotten the words after a few weeks' holiday, but could sing accurately the words of the songs they had been taught before their vacation. I have sometimes set words to music if the children experienced difficulty in remembering instructions. Singing can usually help to improve a child's speech. Allowing the children to sing a descending scale to the syllable 'Boo' is helpful as an aid to articulation.

Carefully selected songs can be adapted for use with the children, e.g. 'Bow wow' by Paul Edmonds, published by Augener, which is suitable for young children, and is especially useful for those who suffer from speech defects. The teacher can sing the song, which is about two dogs. The first is a very friendly young dog, who says 'Bow wow' at intervals. The other dog is rather more inclined to resent intruders and he says 'Bow wow' in a loud voice in order to warn people to keep away. At the appropriate places the children join in saying or singing 'Bow wow'. One half of the group could be the quiet dog, and the remainder of the group could imitate the fierce dog. Some of the children will gradually join the teacher in singing the entire song. When singing, 'his bark is much worse than his bite,' it is preferable to ignor the change in the time values of the fourth and fifth beats, and to sing the notes as six identical beats. Otherwise the very low grade children will be confused by the changing note values at this point.

Fig. 1 Bow Wow

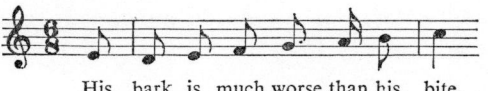

Another useful song for older children, who are either low grade or have speech defects or both, is 'Tambourin', a French folk song, arranged by Gerald Cockshott and published by the Oxford University Press. This is about a rich lady who has beautiful clothes and jewellery. Initially the teacher sings the verse and the youngsters sing 'La la la' at the appropriate places. At a later stage most of the group may be able to sing the entire song. The older girls are usually very interested in this type of song. When teaching the group to sing the 'La la' portion it is advisable to repeat bars 12, 13, 14, and 15 instead of singing bars 16, 17, 18, and 19, as two of the notes sung in

Fig. 2   Tambourin

La,   la, la,   la, la, la,   la, la,   la, la, la,   la.———

bar 14 are omitted in bar 17, and many of the low grade children frequently become confused by very small changes of this type; the corresponding portions of the second and third verses require the same treatment. When teaching the educationally subnormal or the severely subnormal children to sing, the use of a melodic or percussion instrument to accompany the pianoforte introduction to the song, and also between the verses, helps the children to time their entries with greater accuracy. The child playing the introduction is always placed facing the choir in order to provide the singers with both audible and visual assistance. The song 'Tambourin' is a suitable example. The rhythm of the four-bar introduction consists of the repetition of Ann Shirley/Ann Ann/Ann Shirley/Ann Ann.* This could be played on the drums and repeated before each verse, or if desired a different percussion instrument could be used at each repetition.

* See Ch. 4, pp. 34 ff.

The four-bar introduction to 'Edelweiss' from 'The Sound of Music', Rodgers and Hammerstein, published by Williamson Music Ltd., could include a chime bar part for the child who is so low grade that he can only play one chime bar. This also applies in the case of a severely physically handicapped child who, for example, could only make a slight foot or toe movement, but who could play one note using a special aid (see Gadgets). The child would only have to repeat the note twelve times. The advantages are twofold: (a) the children commence singing when the chime bar sounds cease, (b) the very severely handicapped child has the satisfaction of playing an important part in the item.

Fig. 3 Edelweiss

Two Australian aboriginal songs, 'Maranoa Lullaby' and 'Jabbin Jabbin', collected by H. O. Lethbridge, and published by Curwen, can also be used.

These songs are both suitable for the low grade older child, if sung in unison. The melody of 'Maranoa Lullaby' consists of a four-bar phrase which is repeated throughout the song, yet is so well arranged that it never sounds monotonous. The

Fig. 4 Maranoa Lullaby

two-bar introduction is enhanced by the addition of a chime bar repeating the note A six times. This can be played by a child who is too low grade to learn to play more than a single note (see Fig. 4). Near the end of the song the words 'Sleep while mother sings' are followed by one silent bar for the choir, but with the melody of the previous bar repeated on the piano. At this point it is very effective to dispense with the piano part and to let a child play the notes D C A A A on chime bars (see Fig. 5). This also has the effect of ensuring that the children remain silent and only resume the singing after the chime bar sounds have ceased.

Fig. 5   Maranoa Lullaby

Fig. 6   Jabbin

In 'Jabbin Jabbin' a chime bar player could sound F E D E, repeating this from bars 1 to 8 inclusive, in addition to the piano part (see Fig. 6). In bar 11 the chimes F D C could also echo the melody of bar 10 (see Fig. 7). The rhythm of this bar is 'Shirley Ann', and the child has only to play from left to right, although upon one occasion the part was given to a mentally handicapped girl who could only play from right to left, so the chimes were placed in reverse order: C D F.

Fig. 7 Jabbin

Songs that may be a little difficult for some of the subnormal children can be sung by the teacher with an accompaniment arranged for a variety of simple instruments. 'The Little Spanish Town' by Peter Jenkyns, published by Novello, could be arranged in this way. Castanets could be effectively used in the two-bar introduction. There are also a number of breaks in the vocal part where castanets, tambourines, and maracas could be effectively used. On page 4, bars 5, 6, 7, and 8, the lower notes could be played on chime bars (see Fig. 8).

Fig. 8 Little Spanish Town

'Callers', by Arthur Benjamin, published by Boosey and Hawkes, is a lively, attractive song. If used with low grade children the verses could be sung by the teacher, and the children join in at the section referring to 'Cook's friend Emily'. The addition of a G chime bar sounded on the first beat in bars 3, 4, 5, and 6 is effective. On page 2, bar 6, play the notes G, D, B, G, G on a xylophone (see Fig. 9). On page

Fig. 9 Callers

3, bar 10, another child could play the notes B, F♯, D♯, B, B (see Fig. 10), and on page 5, bar 3, a third child could play the notes B♭, F♮, D, B♭, B♭ (see Fig. 11).

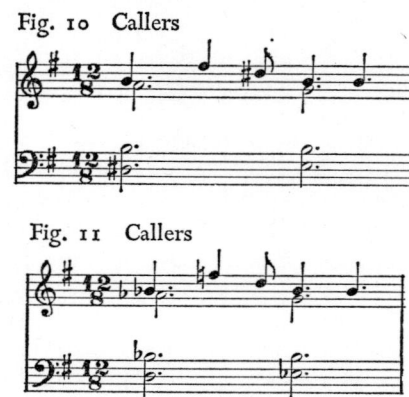

Fig. 10 Callers

Fig. 11 Callers

'Rumba', by Peter Jenkyns (Novello), is a lively modern number with teenage appeal, but when teaching this song to mentally handicapped youngsters the recorder parts had to be omitted and the item sung in unison. There were 24 girls in the 'choir' and they were divided into eight groups with three singers in each group. The result was that, as the verse consisted of eight phrases, no group had to learn more than one phrase (see Fig. 12). The middle section consisted of a short

Fig. 12 Rumba

This tune is not a Min-u-et and Tri-o but a Rum-ba;—
La, la, la, la, la, la, la, la, la, la, la, la, la, la, la...

piano improvisation, followed by a repetition of the first verse. This item gains if castanets, maracas, tambourines, and other instruments can be introduced.

'Slumber Song', by Roger Quilter (Elkin), is a quiet song,

equally suitable for junior or senior educationally subnormal girls. In bars 1 and 2 chime bars C A could be sounded and also on page 3, bars 6 and 7 (see Fig. 13).

Fig. 13 Slumber Song

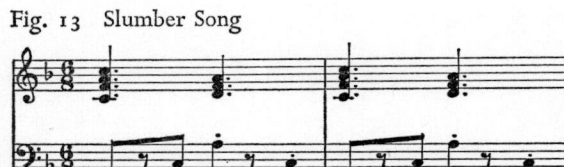

These are just a few examples of how songs can be arranged to include both handicapped vocalists and instrumentalists.

4 Notation

When first devising my system of teaching rhythm to severely subnormal children, I decided that the method most likely to produce quick results would be to use the children's own forenames, as even the very low grade child knows his or her own name, and I always use the children as my 'music'. In the initial stages the children either clap or use percussion instruments. I never use the term 'Percussion Band' except in the case of very small children. The designation 'Instrumental Group' sounds much more important and, except in the case of children whose physical handicap precludes the use of any weighty articles, I always endeavour to obtain full-sized instruments. If you can tell them that the B.B.C. Orchestras use this type of cymbal, etc., they realize that you are not treating them as subnormal citizens. I commence by choosing a child with a single syllable name to be my 'music', e.g. Ann or John. The single syllable name represents the one beat crotchet note. (An explanation of the various music symbols is given on p. 39. Please refer to this when preparing Note Cards for the children.)

The chosen child is seated on one of a row of chairs facing the group. The chairs represent the music stand. I then explain that we are going to play Ann's tune. Then we all clap 'Ann, Ann, Ann, Ann'. The next stage is to play Tune No. 1 in 'Musical Ball Games', by Marion Anderson, published by Cramers, or any similar book of rhythms. The tune consists of crotchet beats. When introducing any new tune or action, play slowly at first, gradually increasing speed as the children make progress; continue until they can perform at the correct speed, otherwise, the lower grade mentally handicapped child will often be slow in understanding your requirements, and the physically handicapped child will frequently experience difficulty in attempting any action involving rapid movements, owing to the nature of his handicap. Therefore, they can only increase speed after a considerable amount of practice. The teacher must judge when each child has reached his or her maximum. In some groups the children's top speed will be considerably slower than that attained by able-bodied children, but in my opinion, if the child is badly handicapped, a substandard result is better than no result. It is much better to try and fail than to refrain from trying if the odds against ultimate success seem unreasonably high. The children clap beats to the music played by the teacher, who repeats 'Ann! Ann!' throughout. Now repeat the tune, but instead of clapping the children use percussion instruments. Then choose another child, e.g. John. This time the children march to 'John! John!' Use the same tune each time, as you are, at the moment, endeavouring to teach rhythm, and the frequent introduction of new tunes would probably result in the child listening to the various melodies instead of concentrating on the rhythms.

Now divide the children into two groups. Group I will sit and play; the second group will march. Then let Group II play and Group I march. Continue until the children can play the crotchet beat with reasonable accuracy. You will, of course, use in turn all the children with single syllable names, as they enjoy being the 'music'. Next, ask the children to repeat 'Ann! Ann!' when clapping, playing or marching. Finally all the mobile children march and play simultaneously as they also say 'Ann!'

It will, naturally, be some time before the children are proficient. Progress will largely depend on the I.Q.s of the members of the group. The original Ann is now placed before the group, and all the children clap her name. Use the same tune. After repeating this exercise once or twice, the teacher should now produce a previously prepared card depicting a blue crotchet note. These notes are easily made by using the gummed circular discs sold by educational suppliers. These are either stuck on postcards or, preferably, on the lined cards used in small filing boxes. The stem of the note is drawn with a coloured pencil or felt pen. Display the card and say: 'This is Ann's picture.' Place the card in Ann's hand and repeat the tune several times. On all future occasions when Ann's tune is played she holds up her picture as a guide to the class. It is important to have a number of these picture cards, each in a different colour. One for every child with a single syllable name! Otherwise you will most likely find yourself in the embarrassing position resulting from a mistake I made in the very early days of my experiments. On one occasion I used a blue crotchet for Ann's picture; this was accepted by the class, but when I played John's tune the next day and showed the same blue crotchet, saying to the children: 'This is John's picture,' John immediately turned to me and rather indignantly said: 'That's Ann's picture, not mine. I'm a boy!' John had been classified as a severely subnormal child; I wonder! From that day onwards I have always used different colours for each child. The next stage is to distribute cards, coloured discs and crayons to the class, and they are helped to make their own pictures of Ann, John, and any other children you have used as 'music'. They first stick the gummed disc on the card, and then draw the stem of the note. The end product will, at first, show little resemblance to the original note, but they will improve with practice and eventually the majority will produce a recognizable picture of 'Ann'.

I next choose a child with a two-syllable name, such as Shirley. The child is seated beside Ann and the group clap, play and march as before to the tune first used. Change the rhythm to Ann, Shirley. Ann = one beat, Shirley = two half beats. When introducing a new note value, always start with the one beat child, immediately followed by the new time division—in this case, Ann Shirley = 1 crotchet beat and 2 quaver half beats. When the children can play the new rhythm correctly, place Shirley on the first seat and Ann on the second. Clap, play and step Shirley Ann = 2 quaver half beats followed by one crotchet beat. Then produce two cards, the first showing Ann's one beat crotchet, and the second card showing Shirley's two half beat quavers. Always give Ann and Shirley their note cards to display when they are included in the music. The children now make pictures of Shirley. In future when introducing a new note value let them clap, play, and step; then show them a picture of the new child, and let them make their own copies. You should test the children by showing a number of cards each depicting Ann or Shirley and ask each child in turn to point to the appropriate picture.

As new names are introduced, add the corresponding pictures of the various sub-divisions of the beat note. Each child is now given the opportunity to choose a picture of either Ann or Shirley for the group to play. The teacher now arranges on a stand cards representing various combinations of Ann and Shirley, e.g. Ann Shirley, Shirley Ann—this equals one beat (Ann) two half beats (Shirley) two half beats (Shirley) one beat (Ann)—Shirley Ann, Shirley Ann, or Ann Shirley, Shirley, Shirley and Ann Ann, Ann Shirley, etc. Then ask individual members of the group to pick out the note cards and arrange their own rhythms for the group to play. Next let half the class play Ann, the other half playing Shirley. Use your right hand when conducting Ann and your left hand for Shirley, thus enabling both groups to play simultaneously.

The child with a three-syllable name is next introduced, e.g. Barbara, or Patricia (each syllable equals one third of a beat); then a four-syllable name such as Elizabeth (each syllable equals one quarter of a beat); and, at a much later stage, Annette (equals one quarter beat followed by a three quarter beat), and then Tweetie the Budgie (equals three quarters of a beat) followed by a quarter beat). Always remember to place Ann, the one beat child, in first place when introducing a child representing a new note value.

The introduction of the tied note (see list of music symbols at the end of this chapter) is most easily accomplished by arranging eight children in a straight line. Choose children with single syllable names. If you are one or two short of the required number, pick out other children and shorten their names, e.g. Patricia could be Pat, and Christine could be Chris.

The children clap 'John, Pat, Jean, Chris, May, Joan, Steve, Dot'. As the members of the group clap you say the names of the children standing, touching each one on the shoulder as you mention his name. Repeat several times until the members are proficient, then ask the two children at the end of the line, Steve and Dot, to hold hands, thus: Steve-Dot. Now explain that when Steve and Dot hold hands you clap 'Steve', but only say 'Dot', without clapping her name. The group will require a little practice, but will soon understand that when two children hold hands you only clap the first of the two names. Now show them the picture of Steve and Dot holding hands. Repeat the clapping with Steve and Dot displaying the picture of the two notes 'holding hands'. Then use the various instruments for further practice.

When introducing a new tune, teach the rhythm before the melody, e.g. if you line up—

Shirley, Mary, Eileen, Jane

—you have the rhythm of

Twinkle Twinkle Little Star

This method will be useful when attempting to overcome the initial difficulty children experience when trying to combine melody and rhythm.

When teaching 'Hot Cross Buns', two groups are required:

       Jane   May   Bob—Dot   (twice)
       Hot   Cross   Buns
       Jenny   Kathy   Mary   Billy
       One   a   Penny   Two   a   Penny
       Jane   May   Bob—Dot
       Hot   Cross   Buns

Rhythm is indicated as follows:

A one-syllable name, e.g. Ann = 1 crotchet beat.

A two-syllable name, e.g. Shirley = 2 quaver half beats.

A three-syllable name, e.g. Barbara, indicates that each syllable equals $\frac{1}{3}$ of a beat.

A four-syllable name, e.g. Elizabeth, indicates that each syllable equals $\frac{1}{4}$ of a beat.

Annette indicates that the short syllable equals $\frac{1}{4}$ of a beat, the longer syllable = $\frac{3}{4}$ of a beat.

Tweetie (The Budgie), the long syllable = $\frac{3}{4}$ of a beat.
The short 'ie' at the end equals the remaining $\frac{1}{4}$ of a beat.

When two children with single-syllable names hold hands, e.g. Tom-Jean, this equals a two-beat note ♩ ♩ or minim ♩ . The children realize that when the notes 'hold hands' the sound is prolonged for two beats. Later the two beat minim note ♩ is introduced and explained.

For the teacher who is unfamiliar with music, an elementary music tutor will provide the necessary background information.

Perhaps one of the most difficult tasks is to teach the children to observe 'rests' (silent beats in the music).

The device I have found most effective is to use little wooden kennels with a plastic dog inside each. First arrange four kennels in a row, and place a dog in each kennel. The four dogs could be named 'Scamp', 'Jock', 'Kim', 'Rex', or any other single-syllable name. Each dog represents a one-beat sound and each empty kennel equals one silent beat. Ask the members of the group if anyone has a dog at home; if the dog's name is suitable, use it. On each kennel the name of its doggy occupant is displayed.

Explain that we are going to clap each dog in turn when I point to its kennel. Let them practise clapping the dogs until they are able to keep accurate time.

You now say Kim is going for a walk to the park. Remove the dog from the third kennel and explain that, as Kim's kennel is empty, we only say her name, but do not clap. Repeat several times, until Kim returns from the park and is back in her kennel. Now clap all the dogs as at first. Jock is the next dog to go for a walk. Point to his empty kennel (the second in the row). They now clap 'Scamp—Kim, Rex'. Continue until Jock returns. The children soon realize that no dog means no clap. Always clap the four dogs several times before removing another animal from its kennel. At a later stage two dogs can be taken for a walk, say Jock and Kim. The children should clap 'Scamp — — Rex' (only SAY the names of the absent dogs). More kennels and dogs can be added if desired, but the introduction of additional dogs should be a gradual process.

Next tell the children that Jock is going for a holiday in Scotland; Jock is, of course, a Scottie. Remove him from his kennel, then tell the group that two puppies are coming to stay in his kennel. The two puppies in the one kennel represent two half beats. Their names are Bim and Bam. The kennels now house Scamp, Bim Bam, Kim, Rex. The dogs again take turns in going walkies. The two puppies should go out together or accompanied by Kim as their mother.

If the children are educationally or severely subnormal, but are mobile, the next stage is to turn the process of learning into a game.

For this you will require four small tables as kennels, two kennel maids, leads and collars for the 'dogs'. The leashes and collars are made from sections of plastic clothes-line in various colours and each lead has a hook. The collars must be fastened around the child's waist, NOT around his neck, to avoid the risk of injury if the kennel maid pulls too violently on the lead. Select four children as 'dogs'. Place them on hands and knees in their 'kennels', and proceed on similar lines to the method used with the plastic dogs. The kennel maid asks a dog to come walkies, and she then fastens the lead to the 'collar' already worn around the child's waist. The dog is then taken to the park, and the other children play their instruments, observing silence when the teacher or helper points to the empty kennel. The first dog returns, and another dog goes walkies.

When you introduce the two 'puppies' representing the half beats, choose the smallest children in the group. When the children have had a considerable amount of practice the two kennel maids each take a dog for a walk, leaving two empty kennels. This game is always thoroughly enjoyed by all the children.

When taking a group of severely subnormal children recently, I was particularly impressed by the behaviour of a twelve-year-old boy whose mental age was between two and three years. When the kennel maid approached him and said: 'Is Scamp coming walkies?', he gave an excellent imitation of an excited dog, jumping up and clawing at her frock, and making it extremely difficult for the girl to attach his lead. They then went for the walk, 'Scamp' pulling hard on the leash in his eagerness to reach the park. When he was brought back to the kennel his mouth was wide open, his tongue hanging out and he was breathing heavily. After re-entering his kennel he lay full length on the floor, settled for a sleep and shut his eyes. Obviously his family possessed a dog, and he had closely observed its reactions to an outing. Although I was assured that he was very dull in most respects, his knowledge of the dog's habits proved beneficial when another set of children became 'dogs' and he joined the musicians. He never failed to observe the silent beat when he saw an empty kennel. I have always found that the use of games, acting, and visual aids of any type speeds up the learning process.

The very badly physically handicapped child can participate in some of the activities described in this chapter, if special care is taken in selecting tasks which are within his very limited capabilities. The almost completely immobile or bedfast child can be used as music and, unless he has a serious speech defect, can repeat 'Ann', etc. Another way in which the child who is unable to use either arms or legs can make a useful contribution is by means of a mouth-controlled device which will enable him to lift the rhythm cards from the rack in which they are stored and to place them on the card stand in the order required for the items to be played by the band (see Appendix A). If the child has lost the use of his hands but is able to use his legs, another attachment enables him to use his feet to play either rhythmic or simple melodic instruments, which are placed on the floor. There are also gadgets which allow the child to make music using his mouth only. If a child cannot hold the note card, attach it to the child's clothing, or thread a ribbon or coloured cord through the card and hang it around the child's neck. The non-ambulant children can sit on chairs and be in the instrumental group, and the ambulant children can march. Those in wheelchairs can, if required, be pushed around, the pusher stepping in time to the music.

When the children are thoroughly familiar with rhythms and the correct symbols for the various note values, this is an opportune time to introduce the staff, the five parallel lines upon which characters denoting the pitch of sounds are written. In the early stages large manuscript sheets measuring 30 × 48 inches (obtainable from the London Music Shop Ltd., 218 Great Portland Street, London W.1) will be found most convenient for use when preparing charts; these are easily fastened to the blackboard by means of large spring clips. Initially it is advisable to use four small sections of the manuscript, preferably mounted on cardboard. The first section only shows the five lines. When their use has been very simply explained, produce section two, which should show a green crotchet (Ann) on the second line of the stave; underneath print in green the name of the note G. The third section consists of a blue crotchet note placed in the space between the second and third lines with the letter A in matching colour. The fourth section shows a red crotchet note with a red letter B below the note.

As the children progress, additional notes can be introduced; but be certain that they are fairly familiar with those already in use before you add to their number. 'Note Tunes', cards showing the notes G, A and B can be placed upon a music stand. When the children can play them correctly, present the same notes in varied order, e.g. GAB, ABG, BAG, GAA, ABB, BAA, GBA, AGB, BGA, GBB, BGG, GBG, AGG, AAB, BGB, GGA, BAB, AAG, GGB, BBA, GAG, AGA, ABA, BBG. The notes GAB have been chosen as being the most useful in the initial stages of pitch reading, because there is a reasonable amount of published recorder music for beginners containing exercises and tunes that only use the notes GAB. These tunes can be played on chime bars, xylophones, glockenspiels, metallophones, pitch pipes, and clarinas, in addition to recorders. When commencing the pitch reading exercises one child will

They Can Make Music

play all the green notes; another child will be responsible for sounding the blue notes and the third youngster will play the red notes. Teach the children to observe that the head of the green note G is in the centre of the second line, that the head of the blue note A is placed in the space between the second and third lines, and that the head of the red note B is in the centre of the third line.

When the youngsters can play a number of simple tunes with each individual being responsible for one note, allow the children to take turns in playing the same tunes, using all three notes. As they become more expert, gradually introduce four, five and six-note tunes, eventually progressing to the complete octave (doh to doh′). Continue using the coloured charts until the youngsters can read and play with a reasonable amount of confidence.

The colour method I used is as follows:

C	(Doh)	Orange
D	(Ray)	Brown
E	(Mi)	Yellow
F	(Fah)	Pink
G	(Soh)	Green
A	(La)	Blue
B	(Ti)	Red

Continue the same sequence as required.

Sharps and flats: a sharp (♯) is a sign which raises a sound half a tone higher, to the next note on the right on the piano keyboard. A flat (♭) is a sign which lowers a sound half a tone, to the next note on the left. These signs are placed in front of the coloured note heads as required. When teaching pitch only use crotchets (Ann). Do not attempt to combine with rhythm until the youngsters are fully conversant with the pitch of the notes. Then introduce the crotchet (Ann), followed by two quavers (Shirley). As soon as they are familiar with this combination of pitch and rhythm proceed to use the crotchet

(Ann) in combination with four semiquavers (Elizabeth), very gradually introducing the remaining note combinations. Immediately the children can read and play from the coloured charts with a degree of fluency, introduce new charts consisting of large black notes—G, A, B, etc.—with the original colours for each of these notes superimposed in the centre of the black ones. This is the transitional stage between using the colours and reading ordinary musical notation, e.g. the note G would be black with a green centre, the note A would be black with a blue centre. When first using the two-colour notes revert to the use of tunes and exercises only using crotchets, gradually progressing to all the other note values and including rests. If necessary, precede the introduction of rests by a recapitulation of the lessons using dogs in kennels.

After a period of using the combined black and coloured centre notes, the children should be ready for the final step. Remove the coloured centres and they will then read from ordinary notation. Continue to use large charts, but only write ordinary notes. The use of big musical symbols for a further period is recommended, as it facilitates reading by slow learners of any grade.

If the youngsters are severely subnormal many of them will not reach the final stages. But do not be discouraged if they are only able to progress a part of the way to musical literacy. If a child is severely subnormal, heavily physically handicapped, or both, to travel part of the way is a real achievement.

The use of this method with the slow learning or the educationally subnormal child will certainly accelerate his progress, and the use of this system of teaching has enabled the very young normal child to read music at an early age.

I devised a very simple method for teaching music to severely handicapped children, described in detail in Appendix A. Claire, a charming and lovable five-year-old, was one of the children I taught by this method. Although her brain was fairly good, she was dumb and quite unable to walk. She had a very limited arm movement and her left arm was extremely weak. In order to induce her to use her arms I made a habit of waving to her whenever I passed the chair on which she sat, but I noticed that she always responded by waving her right hand, so I commenced waving to her with my left hand, but she still always waved her right hand in reply. After some thought, I decided to try waving both hands simultaneously. At first she appeared perplexed by my action, but in a very short time she hesitantly endeavoured to use both arms when waving. Later I informed the Matron about Claire's response and she issued an order that everyone, including the cleaner, should wave both hands each time they passed the child. This action gradually resulted in a considerable improvement in her arm movement.

When commencing her music lesson, she was allotted red as her colour. She was dressed in a red frock, and we played with matching toys. Owing to her lack of speech, the only way we could discover if she was making progress in identifying her colour was to carry her to the form on which the frocks were laid out and then ask her to point to her red frock. She quickly learned to identify her colour, and could also point to any red article in a miscellaneous group of objects. She also became quite proficient in identifying her correct colour when shown half a dozen cards, each of a different colour. She could not pick up her card owing to her limited finger movement, but she made good progress and was soon able to join some of the other children in playing chime bars and pitch pipes. She played the chime bars with the aid of a spring-loaded hammer and a special type of hand grip. The pitch pipe she played was attached to a stand which held it in the correct position. She was gradually able to identify and play tunes using several different colours.

5 Instrumental music

At a very early stage in my work with handicapped children it became apparent that a considerable number of these youngsters would find music-making extremely difficult, if not impossible, unless I devised very simple methods of teaching them and also invented gadgets which would aid them in the actual manipulation of the instruments.

Before the children are able to read from any form of music chart, it is usually possible to teach them to play the melodies of easy tunes by rote, and also to play two or three note accompaniments to simple nursery rhymes, folk songs and other easy vocal items. When starting to teach the children to play melodies, give each child a chime bar and a beater. Arrange the chosen children either standing or seated in a row facing the teacher. A group of eight is a useful number, as this will enable the children to play any tunes between C and the C one octave higher. The tune 'Twinkle Twinkle Little Star' is an example of the type of tune suitable for the early stages of learning.

The teacher who is not a musician should previously have written out the letter names of the tunes she intends to teach the children. Almost any friend with an elementary knowledge of music will be able to assist in the preparation of the letter charts, if the teacher is unable to do so unaided. Alternatively, the teacher should consult a theory book for beginners, where the notes and their letter names will be found. The teacher points to the children in the order in which they should sound their chimes. If the chime is to be played twice, the teacher points to the child a second time. In the song 'Twinkle Twinkle Little Star' the first two notes are C, C, so point twice to the first child. The next two notes are G, G. These are played by the fifth child in the row. This method enables the children to play a recognizable tune within a few minutes and gives them a sense of achievement.

Hohner pitch pipes, which are like a small mouth organ in appearance, can also be used in this way as they can be adjusted to sound any note within an octave, including sharps and flats if required. The sound is produced by blowing. These instruments are rather more expensive than chime bars, but are worth having if funds permit. When using the chime bars to accompany sung melodies very few chimes are required at any one time, as a large number of simple items can be accompanied by only two or three single chimes in the initial stages, progressing to full chords as the children become more proficient.

Here is an accompaniment to 'Three Blind Mice': for this three children are required. Give the first child chime E; the second child chime D; the third child plays chime C. When the other children sing the song, the chimes E, D, C, if continuously repeated in that order, will provide a nice accompaniment. If three more children, with the chimes G, F, E, are added, and the two groups play simultaneously, the result will be even more musical. At a later stage one child could play the three notes E, D, C, and another child play G, F, E, Finally one child using two hammers could play both groups of notes together.

The round 'London's Burning' can be accompanied by the chime bars G and C played as follows:

```
London's Burning    London's Burning
   G        C         G        C

  Fire    Fire      Fire    Fire   etc.
   G       C         G       G
```

Another example of this type of easy, yet effective, accompaniment is 'London Bridge is broken down', chime G, D:

Instrumental music

```
London Bridge is broken down
      G              G

broken down    broken down  etc.
     D              G
```

Music can often be arranged, or specially written, in order to enable severely handicapped children to play together.

One of my early problems arose when I decided to teach the recorder to a group of eight youngsters who, although confined to wheelchairs, apparently had use in their arms and hands. On the first occasion, I discovered that two of the girls suffered from paralysis in one arm. This prevented them from closing all the holes in the recorder simultaneously if required. However, I soon solved this problem by putting gummed paper over half the holes on one of the recorders and letting them play as a pair. The first girl could provide the upper four notes and the other girl played the lower ones, so they were able to join the group. I soon realized that, unless I could improve matters, they would most likely develop an inferiority complex, so I wrote for one of the girls a number of simple solos using the four top notes, with an accompanying part for the two-handed players. I also wrote a similar set of tunes for the other girl.

On another occasion many years ago I had a group of severely subnormal youngsters, some of whom also had fairly severe physical handicaps. On one occasion I staged an Indian scene. In the centre of the floor we placed a huge vase made of cardboard and covered with coloured paper; inside the vase was a boy dressed as a snake. Seated in a circle around the vase were fourteen members of the group, disguised as Indian snake charmers. They each wore a turban made from some brightly coloured material. We were fortunate in obtaining the loan of some coloured curtains. These were draped around the children, completely covering them. Each child in the group had a recorder. As they were quite unable to play these instruments,

I covered certain holes on each recorder, the result being that each child played a different note of the scale. The instrument given to the first child sounded doh, the second child's recorder sounded ray, etc.; the eighth child played top doh, the ninth child sounded ti, the tenth la and so on down to the bottom doh. This routine was repeated half a dozen times. As the snake charmers played the ascending scale, the 'snake' gradually emerged, twisting and turning to the music. When the children played the descending scale, the snake gradually disappeared inside the vase, only to reappear as the musical sounds ascended again. It was fairly easy to teach the children to play in the correct order, as each one commenced to blow his instrument as soon as his neighbour ceased to play. The audience appeared to enjoy this little item, and it is doubtful whether they realized that the recorders had been 'fixed'.

When teaching music to educationally subnormal children, I am naturally anxious to provide opportunities for every member of the group to perform. On one occasion when we were preparing for the school concert, we had at that time a number of low grade children. I was aware of the fact that, unless I could produce something that was very simple and yet would sound good, there was no chance that the children would be able to take part, except perhaps with a percussion band item; but I wanted to give them some kind of music that was above their capabilities. Eventually, I arranged an item in which no child had more than one phrase to learn and play. In order that the members of the audience should not guess that the children were incapable of playing more than one phrase, and also to provide changes in tone colour, I arranged for each phrase to be played by a different instrument, e.g. phrase one—melodica, phrase two—glockenspiel, etc. Later in the piece, when the melodica was again required, a different child played this part. This item was played twice through and was very well received by the audience. This idea could be useful to any of my readers who are faced with a similar problem. I

Above: A group of severely subnormal children. One of the boys playing the Chime Bars is almost blind.

Below: A group of children in a residential home suffering from various disabilities, making music with the aid of a variety of gadgets.

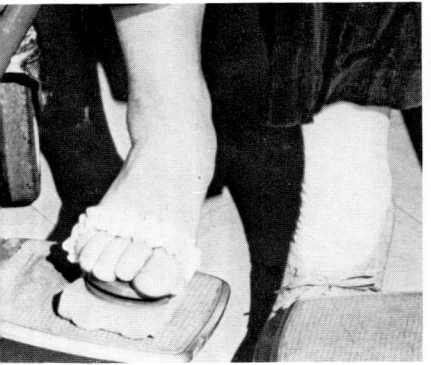
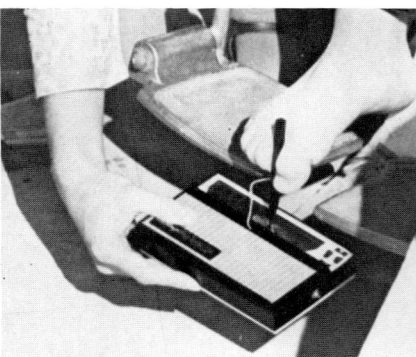

Above left: Foot Castanet with non-skid base.

Above right: Foot-operated Stylophone.

Below: A girl whose arms are paralysed, playing a Clarina with an extended mouthpiece, by means of a plastic 'toe'.

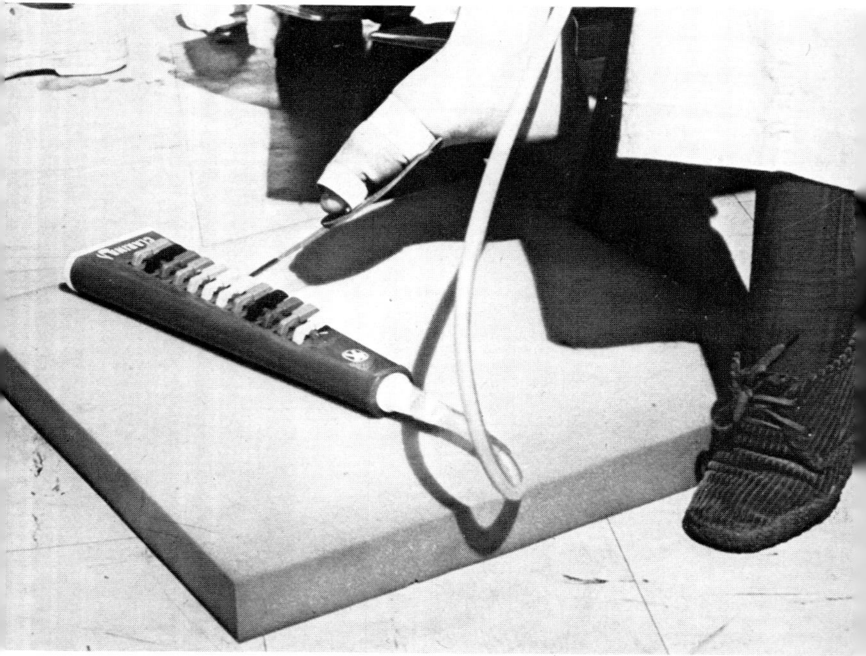

also often use items which are in 'sandwich' form (bread jam bread). This means that after the middle (jam) part has been played, we return to a repetition of the first (bread) part, thus lengthening the item without adding to the children's learning difficulties.

Annette is a severely subnormal nine-year-old girl. Her mental disability is so very great that it proved impossible to teach her to play quite simple tunes, yet she was very interested in music and her ambition was to play a solo at a concert. Rather than disappoint the child, I decided to arrange a short solo for her to play on chime bars. The only possible method was to write a brief ostinato melody, to be repeated six times, with a change of accompaniment for each repetition. Instead of placing the chime bars in the correct order, I arranged them in the order in which each note was to be played, e.g. E, C, A, G, etc. Annette had only to play the notes from left to right, and return to the beginning for each repetition of the melody. With the aid of a simple accompaniment, shared between several children, and with some assistance from the pianist, she played her item at the concert and won quite a lot of applause. This so delighted Annette that she refused to leave the platform until she had repeated her performance; she finally made her exit waving to the audience! This success encouraged her to make a determined effort to learn to play more tunes.

I then planned a slightly more ambitious item for her to perform at the next concert. Although Annette's chime bars were again arranged in the order required, Rita, another girl who had a higher I.Q., was able to play from a simple chart, using the chime bars in the normal way. I allotted the first part to Rita, then Annette played the middle section and Rita repeated the first part, ending with a short 'coda' or 'tailpiece'. The success of the girls' joint effort further increased Annette's interest in music and, although her progress was extremely slow, she persevered and eventually learned to play a number of easy tunes.

They Can Make Music

Certain instruments can be adapted to enable severely subnormal children to play them. For example, I have successfully used the melodica according to the following method, with extremely low grade children.

Take a soprano (green) melodica, and place small green gummed strips on three notes forming a chord. Give the instrument to a child and teach him to place his fingers upon the notes marked in green. Let the child depress the notes and blow, sounding the chord. Follow the same procedure with another child, who has been given an appropriately marked alto (red) melodica. If suitable coloured charts are prepared, a very considerable number of songs can be accompanied by two chords. The coloured strips can be transferred to other notes as required. The example shown below (melodicas) is 'Aunt Rhodie and The Old Grey Goose'. When the children are playing the accompaniment the teacher points to the appropriate circle. Bar 1 is green, so the child holding the green melodica plays the notes bearing the green markings. Bar 2 is also green, so the same child repeats the chord. Bar 3 is red; therefore the child with the red melodica plays. Bar 4 is green, so the green melodica is played. If a song book showing the letters for the guitar chords is used, it is quite easy to make the appropriate charts and to mark the keys on the melodica. This system, although very simple, is quite effective and will enable some of the almost ineducable children to participate.

The auto-harp is a most useful instrument, either for the

The Old Grey Goose

Melodica — F is Doh

Play:	Green	Green	Red	Green	Green	Green	Red	Green
Count:	1 2 3 4	1 2 3 4	1 2 3 4	1 2 3 4	1 2 3 4	1 2 3 4	1 2 3 4	1 2 3 4

The Soprano (Green) melodica plays the green notes (circles)
The Alto (Red) melodica plays the red notes (triangles)

teacher who is not a musician, or for use by children in the class. This stringed instrument can be obtained in three sizes—6 bar, 9 bar, or 12 bar. Always obtain the 12-bar model if possible, as it can produce a larger variety of chords. The bars are mounted on the instrument above the strings and in the centre of each bar is a small button. Each button controls a chord. To produce sounds the player has to press a button and simultaneously to draw a plectrum across the strings. At the end of each bar is the name of the chord controlled by the button, e.g. C major indicates that, when you press this button and strum the strings, you will hear the sound of the C major chord. The other bars are all marked with the appropriate chord. On some foreign makes of auto-harp you may possibly find a different system of marking, but if you consult a musical friend he will soon identify the chords for you and, if you write the English name of each chord on a piece of paper and stick them over the other markings, you will have no difficulty in future identification.

For the teacher who is not a musician the auto-harp, which has a sweet tone, provides an easy way of accompanying herself when singing to the children. The tone of the instrument is very considerably improved if it is placed upon a moderately thick foam rubber mat. When accompanying a soloist, a felt plectrum is recommended, but when accompanying a group of singers use the ordinary type of plectrum, which is usually made of a plastic material. For soft sounds use the strings at the front of the instrument, but if a loud tone is required play upon the other portion, as the greater expanse of the strings increases the volume. Underneath the strings at the front of the instrument will be found the letter names of each note. This enables anyone to play melodies by plucking individual strings. A tuning key is supplied with the instrument, which is fairly easy to keep in tune, but when tuning the strings only make fractional movements of the tuning key, as a jerky movement could break a string.

Many modern editions of folk and other types of songs have guitar chord indications written over or under the notes, e.g. G major indicates the G chord on the guitar; but when playing the auto-harp the performer simply presses the G major button and uses the plectrum to produce the correct sound. The auto-harp also provides the children with a simple method of producing the correct sounds with the minimum effort, thus encouraging them to continue making music. When the harp is played by a child, especially a badly physically or mentally handicapped youngster, put coloured circles on the buttons to be used. Songs like 'Bobby Shaftoe', 'Clementine', and 'One Man Went to Mow' only require two chords, G major and D major, so if the teacher places a green circle on the button marked G, and a brown circle on the button marked D, the child can ignore all the other buttons.

Let the children take turns in accompanying the songs sung by the other members of the group, and let them occasionally have the privilege of accompanying songs sung by the teacher. Commence with songs only requiring one chord, then progress to the two chord tunes as the children grow more proficient. Very many songs can be successfully accompanied by the use of only three different chords. The coloured discs can be transferred to other buttons if required. For blind children braille markings can be placed upon the appropriate buttons and also upon the corresponding charts. For the mentally low grade blind child differing shapes can be attached to the buttons, e.g. square, circle, triangle, etc. When using colour charts the teacher may possibly discover one or two colour blind children in the group. In this event, retain the same colour but use differing shapes. (See p. 52.) Thus the children with normal eyesight will be reading green, red, etc. and the colour blind child will read from triangles, squares, etc. The instruments are frequently placed upon tables or desks, but they can be placed across the child's knees or on the arms of a wheelchair. They are also suitable for a child who can be propped up in bed.

Instrumental music

The chordal dulcimer is an instrument with twelve strings, grouped in four sets of three. Each set sounds a complete chord, usually the doh, ray, soh, fah chords, but all the chords can be varied if necessary. There are two different sized instruments, a soprano and an alto dulcimer. They can be plucked, but are more frequently played with a felt headed beater, which sounds the three notes of the chosen chord simultaneously. They can be used to accompany singing, or can be combined with melodic instruments. They are easy to manipulate, and are very suitable for use by physically or mentally handicapped children. The dulcimer can be placed upon a desk, table, or across a wheelchair. It can also be played by some children who are confined to bed. It can be played with extended beaters, T-shaped beaters, spring-loaded beaters, and powered beaters; other types can be made to fit in with the special requirements of individual children. (See Appendix A.) When using this instrument with educationally subnormal children, it is advisable to place a white disc under each chord, bearing the number of the chords, e.g. 1 (doh), 2 (ray), 5 (soh), 4 (fah). The children can then quickly learn to play from number charts. The severely subnormal child, and the very young child with a normal brain, will usually respond to colours. Place coloured discs under each chord, e.g. orange = doh, brown = ray, pink = fah, green = soh. They can then learn to play from coloured charts. Many simple songs only require two or three chords; therefore, within a short period they can combine with others to provide a simple accompaniment for the singers.

The mini bass or bass D is a useful addition to the elementary instrumental group. It has four strings which are pitched one octave lower than the chordal dulcimer. It is a good foundation instrument and can be played by a child with only one hand, or by a child with very short arms if an extended plectrum is provided. In both cases a stand to hold the instrument is necessary. It can also be placed across a wheelchair, or could be used in a hospital ward. Some of the severely sub-normal children can be taught to play this instrument if coloured discs are placed under each string, e.g. the bass is tuned as follows: C = orange, G = green, D = brown, F = pink, and the children play from charts using the same colours. This type of chart enables the children to combine with other instrumentalists. If the player can only use one hand, or if the child's fingers are too weak to press the strings, these instruments can be played either in pairs or in groups of four, restrung as follows: instrument No. 1 has its strings tuned to C, D, E, F; the strings on instrument No. 2 are tuned to G, A, B, C (see mini bass, pp. 81–2). Thus the two instruments, if used in combination, are tuned from bottom doh to top doh in the key of C major. If four basses are available, the other two are tuned in the scale of G major. Therefore, the children could accompany a song in the key of C by using instruments 1 and 2; if the middle part of the song is in key G the other pair of instruments is used for this portion. They are also useful for playing simple instrumental solos. The basses can, of course, be retuned by the teacher if required in the minor or in any adjacent keys. These instruments can be made with or without frets.

Many ordinary musical instruments can be modified or adapted to enable physically handicapped children to play them. Of course, the majority of instruments can be played by a person confined to a wheelchair, although some modifications will be required in certain cases. For example, if the fingers on a child's left hand are too weak to press the strings on a violin or similar instrument, it may be possible to solve the problem by reversing both bridge and sound-post and restringing the violin in the opposite direction; i.e. instead of G D A E, arrange in reverse order, E A D G. The child will then bow with the left hand and press the strings with the fingers of his more capable right hand. I have found this method has invariably been successful in solving the problem. The use of the weak arm for bowing has had the effect of exercising and strengthening the muscles. A number of instruments such as the trumpet can also be played by a one-armed musician. The provision of specially designed stands to support the instruments may be necessary in some cases (see Appendix A).

A choral or orchestral conductor in a wheelchair is most certainly a practical proposition. A larger and higher podium, with a ramp instead of steps, and the provision of a fairly long baton would overcome the disadvantages of a conductor who remains seated throughout a performance. The percussion player can, if necessary, have a special type of drumsticks, and other devices can be provided to help him to overcome any difficulties he may encounter (see Appendix A). If the non-ambulant player can join an ordinary orchestra, this will be the ideal solution to most of his problems, as the handicapped person can choose any instrument within his capacity, and the instruments presenting very great difficulties to the wheelchair player, such as the double bass, can be played by those members who have full use of all their limbs.

I have not mentioned vocal music, as this is, of course, possible for all handicapped persons, unless they suffer from a vocal or speech defect. In fact, some people who cannot speak can sing, and it is a well-known fact that persons who stammer when speaking can overcome this defect when singing.

Megan, a physically handicapped 15-year-old, has only one finger of her left hand, but her other hand is normal. She is now learning to play a suitably adapted organ. This organ has a device which will enable the player to produce a major or minor chord by depressing one note, but the performer can also have a plastic 'finger' attached to his hand thus enabling him to produce other notes. This is brought into action by forearm rotation.

Clive is physically handicapped through an accident. One half of his right hand has been removed, but thanks to a major adaptation to his saxophone and flute he is now able to continue his studies. The keys of the saxophone have been placed in a double row near the top of the instrument. The second row of keys are connected by brass rods to the appropriate positions. The flute is a somewhat similar adaptation.

David is another accident case, aged seventeen. He was a member of a beat group, but found he could not play his saxophone as he had to wear a plaster support. Fortunately, I was able to suggest another instrument which was much easier for him to manipulate.

Furthermore, I have devised numerous special gadgets which make it possible for badly handicapped children to make some kind of music. A list of these is included in Appendix A.

Each gadget was originally devised to aid a particular child and later modified to conform to the special needs of other children. In addition to the aids described in the Appendix, I am still working on new devices and improvements to the existing gadgets. I have listed the gadgets I have found especially useful for children with various types of disability, e.g. for those who have use in only one arm, etc. These will serve as a general guide, but many of these aids will also be useful for those suffering from other handicaps.

Jean, a nine-year-old Thalidomide child, had only very tiny arms with two small digitals on each arm. Her problem was to find an instrument suitable for her to play. The solution was the provision of foot gadgets which would allow her the choice of playing any one of three different instruments.

Christine was an 8-year-old Thalidomide girl whose difficulty is common to many such children. She wished to play a recorder, but only possessed one usable finger on each hand; the provision of a clarina on a special stand to hold the instrument enabled her to join the school recorder group.

Fred, aged 12, was a physically handicapped boy. He had only one usable arm and, like Christine, wished to play the recorder. When I recommended a three-hole folk pipe he found this solved his problem.

George was a twelve-year-old Muscular Dystrophy case. For

a considerable period he was able to play the drum, not only with his companions in the unit, but also when listening to recordings of 'pop' tunes. He really imagined that he was a member of the group. As his disease progressed he gradually lost the ability to make the necessary arm movement; he also experienced gradually increasing difficulty in holding the drumsticks. Fortunately, I had a ready-made solution to his problems. I had, some time previously, designed a powered drumstick with an attachment which secured it firmly to the hand, so by providing suitable arm rests to support his gradually deteriorating limbs he was able to enjoy his participation in music for a much longer period than would have been possible without the aid.

Another problem arose when a boy who was paralysed in both arms expressed a desire to play a xylophone. To enable him to play, I devised two small powered beaters. These were attached to his shoes. The xylophone was placed upon the floor and he was able to play, using his feet instead of his hands.

I have on numerous occasions had to cater for children suffering from erratic hand movements. My solution to some of the children's difficulties was to provide them with sets of chime bars with each note in triplicate, e.g. if three chime bars are placed in front of the child, he aims for the middle one and will probably hit one of those on either side but he will produce the correct sound. I have also had xylophone notes made each measuring about 10 × 10 inches. A child with quite a considerable amount of uncontrollable movement can usually play notes this size. Of course, he could not manage a full range of notes this size, but if he is given three bass notes sounding, doh, fah, soh respectively, he can provide an accompaniment to the other instruments. This limited participation in the music can be quite important, if you choose either songs or instrumental items suitable for a doh fah soh bass.

Appendix A gives a detailed list of these gadgets, arranged

both according to the child's handicap and according to the type of instrument. Of course, this is not an exhaustive list; each child has an individual problem which calls for its own solution. But I hope that an account of the gadgets I have found useful will give the reader ideas for thinking up many new ones.

6 Other musical activities

It is enormously important for the children's psychological welfare that they should not be left out of any musical (or, indeed, any) activity if they can possibly be included. A little ingenuity will often reveal ways of including even the most helpless children in all sorts of musical activities.

On one occasion we had five little children, of whom all were completely helpless and two were also dumb. How to include these children in a concert was a rather difficult problem. The solution was to arrange for the choir to sing several items in a 'garden'. Grass-green paper spread upon the floor provided the 'lawn'. Artificial flowers were 'planted' around the platform and the five children dressed as gnomes were arranged sitting cross-legged in the garden. By their inclusion we had given joy to these children, who missed so many pleasures taken for granted by the normally fit child.

Elsewhere upon another occasion I utilized the idea of a garden to enable us to include a completely immobile teenage girl, who sat in a deckchair and sang a solo. The only other occupant of the garden was a lad who could only move about by the use of walking aids. He was dressed as a gardener and supported himself by leaning on a spade. The girl's solo was followed by a duet between herself and the gardener.

Musical plays are very useful if you are teaching physically handicapped children. The child's physical defects can often be concealed if he is given a part in which he can wear flowing robes. The completely immobile child can be costumed, seated on a chair, and sing or speak as required. The mobile children can take the more active roles.

They Can Make Music

Sarina, a helpless six-year-old child without use in either arms or legs, was normally strapped in a wheelchair and was a member of the audience whenever other less handicapped members of her unit staged a show. However, after much thought, it was decided to let her take the part of a puppet in a forthcoming entertainment. She was dressed in a blue frock; around her waist was a yellow sash with a large bow. She also wore a matching head band and socks with blue shoes. The sash was the only way to disguise the fact that, without a support, she would have fallen off the chair. The seat used was covered in non-skid material and she was placed on the chair; the sash was then securely fastened to the back of the seat, thus acting as a 'safety belt'. On her wrists, legs and ankles she wore fancy garters with bells attached. When her face was made up she appeared to be a large doll. The strings were partly concealed under the garters and, owing to the fact that her limbs were extremely limp, she made a perfect puppet. When the puppeteer, a handicapped senior child, whose own disabilities were concealed by the screen, manipulated the strings and her legs and arms moved in different directions, the child's obvious delight was ample reward for the effort that had been made to include her in the display.

A wax-works is a very useful item. Any child, however badly disabled, can be dressed up and become a wax figure. Children in wheelchairs can be covered with flowing robes. A boy who has only one leg can be a pirate. A child who is compelled to remain in a recumbent position can be given a suitable character to represent, and if costumed for the part the audience will not realize why the child is lying on a couch or whatever you use as a substitute. The mobile children can be visitors, and if several of the wax figures represent musicians—either pop stars or the great classical musicians—a child could approach one of the figures and say: 'Look, there's Sir Harry Lauder; his most famous song was "I love a Lassie". Let's sing it now.' The children then sing a verse or two of the song.

They continue to examine the figures and then discuss another musician. This will allow the group to sing again.

Do not hesitate to omit or alter parts in published works. If you have the slightest doubt about infringement of copyright, contact the publishers and explain that you wish to simplify the piece in order to make it possible for handicapped children to perform it. They are almost certain to allow you to modify it. In some cases there is no need to worry. As an example of very minor alterations that I have myself made, I recall an occasion when, just before Christmas, I was rehearsing a group of very low grade teenagers, who were going to sing a Christmas story with a percussion accompaniment. I found that several of the songs were beyond the capacity of the children, so I substituted very well-known carols where necessary.

On some occasions you may have to make alterations to a few of the actions and change some of the wording to tailor the parts to fit the children's needs. In a children's Christmas play there is one scene where two little boys and two small girls are running around a bedroom, wearing nighties and pyjamas. Their mother comes in and says: 'Why aren't you in bed yet? Father Christmas won't come unless you go to sleep quickly.' As two of the children in the play were immobile they were placed in their cots before the curtains were opened and the mother enters and says: 'What! Aren't you asleep yet? Father Christmas . . . etc.'

Frequently a slight alteration here and there makes it possible to include some children who are too handicapped to take part otherwise.

In a fairy story there is no reason why the Princess should not have accidentally fallen down some steps and hurt her leg, so that she will have to walk with the aid of two sticks or crutches until her leg gets better!—or she could, if necessary, be in a wheelchair. Make the situation fit in with the child's disability. Do not take the easier way by only choosing children who can act according to the original script.

When visiting a hospital, I met Denise, a young teenage girl who had been involved in an accident. As a result of her injuries, she was compelled to lie flat on her back. At the time of my visit, arrangements were being made for a Christmas show to be given by some of the young patients. I asked the producer if Denise would be included in the show: 'Of course not. It would be impossible to include anyone who is unable to sit up,' replied the producer. I explained that unless there was any special medical reason why her bed must not be moved, the script could be amended to include a bedroom scene, and that her bed could be wheeled on to the stage and Denise given a speaking part. An explanation of why she could not yet sit up could be included in the script. I stressed the fact that, as she was so helpless, this gave added importance to her inclusion, which would certainly raise her morale. I am pleased to report that, after some hesitation, the producer agreed to modify the play and to include Denise.

A colleague of mine who was in charge of a home for severely disabled children invited me to witness their Christmas show. Her charges included a small group of very badly disabled children who were also dumb. My colleague was determined that these children should all be included in the show. They were dressed up as angels, complete with white robes, wings and halos. On the occasion of the final rehearsal, the real choir sang all the carols, which were taped and at the actual performance the tape recorder was placed out of sight behind the 'angels', who tried to mime the carols. Their delight at being dressed up as angels and participating in the Christmas show more than justified the artifice which had made their appearance possible.

When possible combine the severely subnormal children with normal youngsters. If you are preparing your group for a concert or a play, teach the very simple parts to your children, and ask the Head of the nearest school for normal children if his or her youngsters will learn the difficult parts and augment your group on the occasion of the performance. You will usually find that the Head and the youngsters themselves will be quite co-operative.

The severely subnormal children learn to sing a simple melody, and the vocal harmony is sung by the normal children. The result of their combined efforts is a good concert. The subnormal child will understand if you say they were all very good, but will not realize just how much of their success is due to the assistance they received from the other children. The result will raise the morale of the subnormal youngsters and inspire them to make further efforts. If the other school possesses an instrumental group, you may obtain their services as a backing group for the choir. It is also sometimes possible to teach subnormal children to play some very simple instrumental items and to obtain the co-operation of the nearest school for physically handicapped children. Many of these youngsters have normal brains and the members of their instrumental group may be willing to combine in rehearsals for a joint concert. This effort would be beneficial to both groups. The subnormal children enjoy the combined music making, and the physically handicapped youngsters realize that they are helping other children who are even more handicapped than themselves.

Some years ago I watched two groups of boys, all using crutches, yet able to play football with the utmost confidence and at a speed which appeared almost incredible to the ordinary onlooker. Watching the footballers prompted the thought that, if badly handicapped lads can successfully play football, there is no reason why youngsters confined to wheelchairs cannot learn to dance; and I recalled many conversations with older non-ambulant people, who had said that, when they were teenagers, they had often longed to dance, especially when watching their more fortunate companions enjoying this sociable form of recreation. As a result of this experience, I began to consider the possibility of selecting dances suitable for people in wheelchairs, and experience has proved that this is a practical proposition, as a considerable number of folk and square dances can be adapted to enable youngsters to enjoy a modified form of dancing.

A large room is essential, as wheelchairs require a considerable amount of room in which to manoeuvre if the risk of collision, or injury to the dancers' hands or feet, is to be minimized. If a large room is not available, the dancers must only participate in small groups, and in some cases it may be necessary only to permit clockwise movement. When performing the dances, care must be taken to ensure that the participants do not get unduly fatigued. Those in self-propelled chairs will soon discover that their arms quickly tire with the unaccustomed continuous movement. The electrically propelled chairs are fairly easy to manoeuvre for considerable periods, and so are those pushed by an attendant or any other fit person available although the people pushing the chairs may get exhausted unless allowed occasional rests! In the early stages it is usually desirable to have 'pushers' for all the chairs.

Before commencing, divide the dancers into two groups. Each group should only participate in alternate dances. This method will help to ensure that no one is overtired, and will also allow those dancing a larger space in which to manoeuvre their chairs.

The music must be played at a speed considerably slower than the normal tempo, until the dancers learn the various movements and can execute them with a fair amount of precision. In any case, since chairs are usually slower than ordinary dancers, it will probably be necessary to play the music at a slower tempo, or—if using records—to allow twice the amount of music.

Initially, practise with small groups (a) moving in time, (b) turning, travelling from corner to corner, (c) moving in pairs, (d) moving forwards and reversing to their original positions,

Above: Sheena, aged 6 (recovering from severe burns), playing the Auto-harp.

Below: John (who lost his arm in an accident) playing the bowed Psaltery.

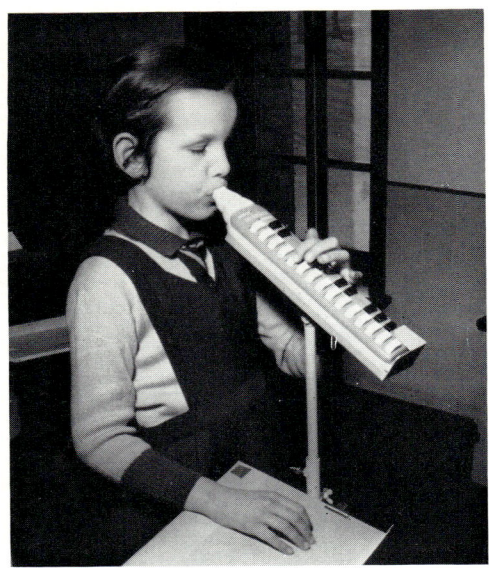

Above: Ruth, aged 7, has a special stand enabling her to play the Melodica and read braille music simultaneously.

Below: Gary plays the trumpet with the aid of a stand which holds the instrument.

(e) two groups crossing from opposite corners simultaneously, allowing sufficient space for the chairs to cross in the centre, (f) simple follow-my leader, (g) two groups forming an inner and an outer circle, moving in opposite directions, and (h) a figure-of-eight.

At first use a member of staff as leader for each group. Later the dancers can take turns as group leaders. If well-known music is chosen, the dancers will follow with greater ease. When the dancers are familiar with some or all of the movements, you can then begin to incorporate a few of them into simple dances, gradually increasing the variety and difficulty as the dancers grow more proficient.

As wheelchairs require extra time when turning it is usually better to divide the dancers into two or three groups; e.g. Group I could move from one side of the room to the opposite side. They could then turn in a leisurely fashion and await their turn to return to the base. Whilst the Group I dancers are turning, Group II may be crossing from corner to corner, or travelling around in a circle, or groups of dancers could be placed in two straight lines with a pair of dancers travelling between the two lines of wheelchairs. It is advisable to start with simple movements, and gradually build up the dances as the youngsters become more familiar with the various changes of position. This method of dividing the movements is much easier for the dancers to memorize and to perform.

Owing to the variety of disabilities often encountered within the same group, it is frequently impossible to adhere strictly to all the movements normally associated with each dance. It may, therefore, be necessary to 'borrow' parts from two or three dances, in order to make up one dance in which all can participate. As with many other activities for the handicapped, the person organizing the dances must be an adept in the art of improvisation. Thus I have thought it best to leave the form of the dances to the organizer, after he or she has experimented with the group, as it is impossible to select dances that will be suitable for all types of handicapped people. So I have tried to give some hints and examples of various movements which can be moulded into dances; the final choice of material lies with the person in charge of each group.

Do try to include as many people as possible, as the dancers will derive considerable benefit from mixing with others, working as a team or with a partner. This is an enjoyable social activity, giving the participants a chance to meet and dance with a variety of people. Those who use self-propelled wheelchairs are also helping to strengthen their muscles. Others not in self-propelled chairs may be able to make arm and hand movements such as clapping, touching their partners as they pass each other, or holding hands as two wheelchairs are pushed along together. In some of the dances they can frequently change places and greet each new associate as they team up together. If it is possible to form your own band, this will add to the pleasure of the group. In any case some members of the unit will be able to play castas, etc. in addition to any instruments that may already be in use.

One of our difficulties arose from a request by some members of the group who were able to move about, using various walking aids, and travelling at different speeds, but who desired to join in the dancing. The immediate solution was to remove the completely non-ambulant youngsters from their wheelchairs and replace them with the semi-ambulant teenagers. These young people found that the novelty of joining in a wheelchair dance was a really exciting experience, and we had to repeat this process at frequent intervals. However, with very careful planning and selection, it is not impossible to arrange a few very simple dances suitable for those using walking aids. The speed of the movements has to be reduced to the tempo of the slowest of the semi-ambulant youngsters. Sometimes the same dance may have to be repeated at three different speeds to enable all the young people to take part.

If normally fit young people would be available as partners

for these semi-disabled youngsters, this would not only give considerable pleasure to the handicapped dancers, but the fit teenagers could also guide and steady the disabled dancers when required. It is also quite possible for persons confined to wheelchairs to join mobile, physically fit young folk in many square and folk dances. Slight modification will be required to allow for the fact that the wheelchair cannot turn as rapidly as an ordinary dancer, although some young folk are amazingly skilful at manoeuvring their chairs. Naturally this ability varies according to the nature and severity of the youngster's disability, but those with approximately normal arm movement and intelligence can compare quite favourably with the physically fit youngsters.

There is not the slightest doubt that they will all derive great pleasure from this form of recreational activity and that, if pursued in moderation, it is also good exercise and has considerable psychological value. Those children forced to lie on their backs in spinal carriages and even those who lie face downwards can be wheeled around with the others, and have the joy of taking part in a pleasurable group event. Do try and make it possible for the majority of youngsters to join in the fun.

The excellent results obtained through using music as an aid to the development of the handicapped child prompted my experiments in using music as an aid to the teaching of other subjects. The reader will recall my previous statement that music helps to arouse the child and, when allied to words, aids the memory. Therefore, it was only logical to utilize music in the teaching of other subjects. Although my experiments in this field are not yet complete, the response from the children has fully justified the introduction of some rather unusual methods of teaching. Several subjects have already been successfully attempted and others are still in the planning and experimental stage.

I have found the introduction of a series of simple musical

lesson-games speeds up the process of teaching educationally subnormal children, and also enables the severely subnormal child to acquire an elementary knowledge of a variety of subjects. Although many of these lesson-games were originally planned for mentally and/or slightly physically handicapped children, it is possible to use the same methods, with slight variations, for really badly physically handicapped youngsters, and there is no doubt that lesson-games definitely provide motivation for the child with stiff limbs to make every effort to use them.

In most games children in wheelchairs, even those in spinal carriages, can be moved around by attendants, or possibly by other children. (The child in a self-propelled chair is, of course, no problem.) This method enables all members of the group to participate with the more mobile children on more or less equal terms. Obviously a reasonable amount of space is required, especially if the children are in wheelchairs. Some suggestions for adapting many of the games to permit the inclusion of almost immobile children are included in the instructions for a number of the lessons. The system is outlined in Appendix C.

These are just some of the ways in which music can be used to help handicapped children. I hope that the dedicated teacher will be inspired by my findings to attempt new solutions to his children's unique problems.

In conclusion I quote two extracts from a letter written by the late Andrew Carnegie on August 2nd, 1903, containing instructions to the trustees, as I consider the advice contained therein is equally relevant to those who are contemplating teaching the handicapped child:

> Remember you are pioneers, and do not be afraid of making mistakes; those who never make mistakes never make anything. Try many things freely, but discard just as freely.

> Do not put before their first step that which they cannot take easily, but always that which leads upwards.

Appendix A

Gadgets

(i) Arranged according to handicap
(explanatory details will be found in list (ii))

For a person with use in one hand only
Three-hole folk pipe
Specially adapted casta
Double-headed drumstick
Bowed psaltery
Guiro on a special stand
Specially designed gadget to enable a child with only two
   fingers on one hand to use a tape recorder

Foot-controlled
Electronic organ
Toe-operated stylophone
Foot-operated castas
Foot-operated battery hammers
Foot-operated spring hammer for chordal dulcimer
Foot-operated spring hammer for chime bars
Foot-operated tom-tom
Foot-operated cymbals
Foot- and mouth-controlled clarina
Foot- and mouth-controlled melodica
Foot-operated bass drum

For the blind or partially sighted
Stand to hold various instruments
Adjustable music holder

Auto-harp with 6 different shapes for chords
Roller stand with strip lighting and magnifier and a reversible motor
Similar device taking enlarged music
Anglepoise music stand

Head- or mouth-operated
Mouth casta
Head casta
Mouth-controlled electronic organ
Mouth-controlled battery hammer
Head-controlled battery hammer
Head-controlled spring hammer for xylophone, etc.
Head-controlled spring hammer for chordal dulcimer
Mouth-operated record player
Mouth-operated 'Devil's pitchfork'
Mouth-operated plectrum
Mouth-controlled stylophone
Mouth- and foot-controlled clarina
Mouth- and foot-controlled melodica

For Thalidomide children
Adapted kalimba
Screw-on extensions for the manipulation of instruments
'Fingers' attached to hands or feet
Mouth plectrum
Special finger-grip plectrum
Extended plectrums
Melodica or clarina stand
Tape recorder manipulator
Stylophone attachments

Therapeutic Aids

For Forearm Rotation
Clockwork musical box

When wound the musical box plays. After the tune has ended, a 'Jack-in-the-box' pops up. The child enjoys playing with the toy, and the winding action causes forearm rotation.

Double-headed drumstick

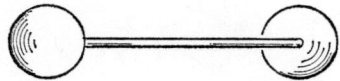

'Rainmaker' drum

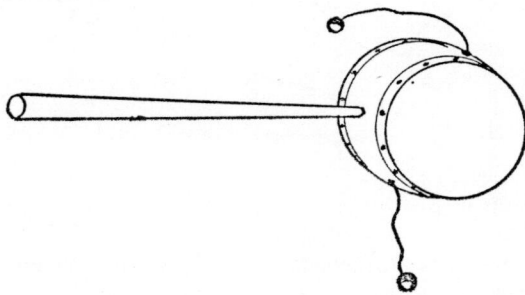

For Wrist Flexibility
Hand bells (for the older child)
Small bells (for the young child)
Castanet with handles
Maracas

For Foot and Leg Movement
Foot-operated casta
Knee casta

Casta attached to the ankles

An instrument specially designed for a boy whose feet were flexed on tip-toe. A hinged sandal mounted on a frame and normally in a tip-toe position. By pressing his heel down a quarter of an inch the child makes an electrical contact

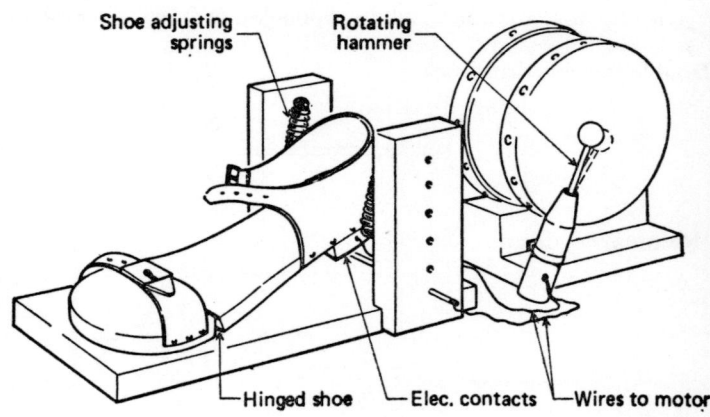

resulting in a drum beat or other musical sound. The contact bar can be moved downwards as the child's heel movement improves. It is essential for the child to produce different sounds with each foot, otherwise he would only exercise the one he could move with the least effort. This appliance can be adjusted to produce a variety of sounds and thus retain the child's interest.

A gadget for playing various instruments with the foot.

A flat base with electric contact points at each end, activated by the heel and toe movements of the patient. These movements not only operate musical instruments, but also help to develop flexibility in the knees and ankles, and to strengthen some of the leg muscles. The instruments used with this aid are interchangeable.

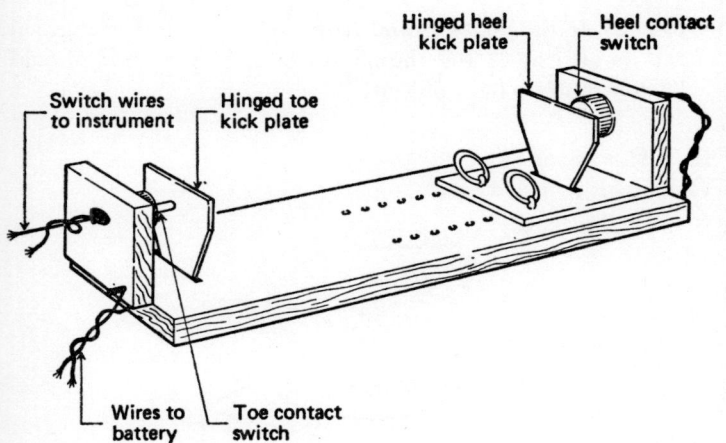

Finger movement and strength

Kalimba

Hand casta

Castanet attached to the hand

Produces sounds with the minimum finger movement, and cannot be dropped. Can be used in conjunction with suitable records.

Glove with attachments

For a child with slight thumb movement only; musical

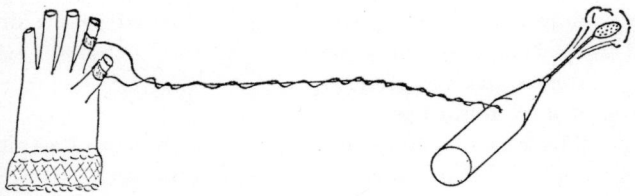

sounds are produced when the child makes very small inward and outward movements of the thumb. This induces the child to try and make the changes of position required to activate the contacts and helps to extend and strengthen the movement of the thumb. Eventually the child should be able to grasp light objects.

Arm Movement
Casta with non-skid base

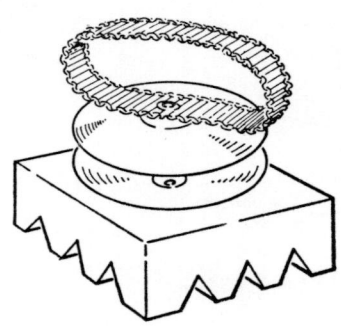

Bowed psaltery (either arm)
Guiro (either arm)

(ii) Arranged according to type of instrument
PERCUSSION INSTRUMENTS

1. 'Rainmaker' drum
   This is a circular drum with a handle. Sound is produced by two beads which are attached to the drum by short cords. The beads strike the instrument when the handle is rotated rapidly.
2. Rotary tom-toms
   These can be adapted for tuning by means of a 'pitchfork'. This method makes possible the accurate tuning of these instruments, when the child's hand disability is too great for the normal method of tuning to be practicable. The tom-tom can be played with a powered beater if required.

3. Rotary drum

    This can also be tuned by the use of the 'pitchfork', but a small alteration to the normal stand is also necessary. This type of drum can be played with a powered drumstick, with extension if required.

4. Hand casta

    This type of castanet is definitely easier for the handicapped child, as it can be used by youngsters who are without the ability to grip or to make any finger movement.

5. Adapted casta

    This hand casta has been adapted for the child who can only use one arm, and has a non-skid base which also acts as an insulator.

6. Knee casta

    This is another variation that is attached to the child's legs just above the knees.

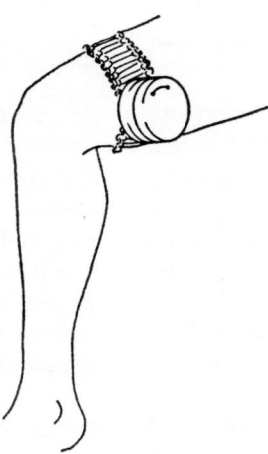

7. Foot casta

    This is intended for use by a child whose arms are

paralysed. It has a non-skid base and is attached to the child's foot by a band of coloured garter elastic.

8. Ankle casta

    This is attached to the child's ankles in a similar manner to no. 7.

BEATERS FOR PERCUSSION INSTRUMENTS

9. Double-headed drumstick

    This aid is intended for a child who can only use one arm, as it serves the dual purpose of enabling the percussionist to play ordinary beats and also to obtain a fast roll by rapid rotation of the wrist.

10. Powered drumstick

    This aid consists of a small electric motor to which is attached a revolving drumstick. It is powered by a small battery and the drumsticks rotate at speed when

    the motor is switched on. This gadget is secured to the child's hand by means of a piece of garter elastic and is suitable for those without grip or arm movement.

11. Foot-operated powered drumstick

    This is a similar aid and is intended for use by children whose arms are paralysed. It will enable a child to play xylophones, etc., if the instruments are placed upon the floor. The hammers are attached to his feet and the child plays by using his feet instead of his hands.

12. Balanced hammer

    This is a perfectly balanced long hammer with a weighted end, and will enable a child with minimum wrist movement to play chime bars, dulcimers, and other instruments.

13. Spring hammer
    Another type of hammer incorporating a spring and with a felt head. This enables a child with similar difficulties to play the chordal dulcimer (a stringed instrument).
14. T-shaped hammer
    This hammer is designed to enable children who cannot move the arm forwards or backwards to surmount this difficulty. The various chords on a chordal dulcimer are played by a sideways movement of the forearm. When using this hammer the player sits facing the end of the instrument. Avoid the end containing the tuning-pins, as this will tend to obstruct the movements of the hammer.
15. This is another battery-operated gadget with a special type of head and is also a useful aid for the performer on the chordal dulcimer, as it will simultaneously play any two strings a fifth apart and also gives a kind of vibrato effect.
16. Extensions for battery-powered hammers
    Extensions of various shapes and sizes have been designed for children in wheelchairs.
17. Hand-controlled powered hammers
    This type of hammer can be used by children without normal arm movement.
18. Special beaters
    These are intended for use by Thalidomide and other children with deformed arms. They are long-handled beaters of various types.
19. Extensions
    Screw-on extensions can be provided as required by children suffering from a variety of physical disabilities.

MELODIC INSTRUMENTS

20. Bowed psaltery
    This instrument can be used as a substitute for the

violin and can be played by a child who has only one arm. Each note can be individually tuned and the disadvantage of not being able to lift the instrument has been overcome by providing it with legs. If placed upon a table, there is no muffling or distortion of the sounds. It can be bowed by either the right or the left hand. If the child's hand is weak, a small cello bow will help to compensate for lack of arm and hand pressure.

21. Three-hole folk pipe

    The three-hole pipe will enable a child with only one hand to play many simple tunes.

22. Guiro

    This simple bamboo instrument, if firmly mounted on a suitable non-skid base, can easily be manipulated by a child with only one arm. If the child's fingers are weak and he cannot grip the stick firmly, the addition of an elastic band secured to the stick, put over the child's hand, overcomes the difficulty.

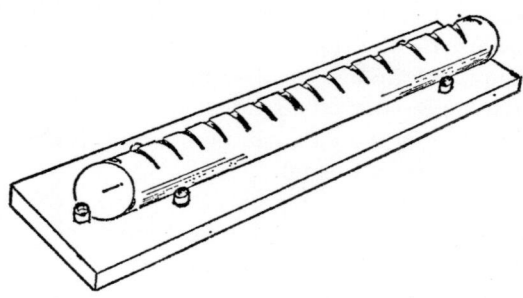

23. Kalimba

    This dulcet-toned instrument consists of a number of metal keys mounted on a box resonator, producing a harmony of accordant sounds when the keys are 'stroked' with fingers or thumbs. This instrument is especially suitable for the low grade mentally handicapped child.

24. Auto-harp

   The auto-harp is a small stringed instrument and has, in addition to the normal strings upon which melodies can be played, a set of up to twelve buttons, placed upon cross bars. When the player depresses a bar with one hand and simultaneously strums the plectrum over the strings, the harp will sound the complete chord indicated on the bar that has been depressed, e.g. if you press the button marked C major, your strum will produce the sounds appropriate to the chord of C major. This instrument is very useful for the teacher who is not a musician.

25. Adapted harp

   This has weighted buttons for easy operation by children with weak fingers and arms.

26. Another type of adapted harp

   This auto-harp is fitted with a number of buttons, each of a different shape. This enables the very low grade blind child, who cannot be taught to read braille, but who can be taught to distinguish the various shapes, to play this instrument.

27. Foot-operated clarina

   The foot-operated clarina is an adaptation for children whose arms are paralysed. The mouth-piece is connected to the instrument with flexible plastic tubing. The instrument is on a non-skid base and is played by means of plastic toes (see no. 43). A stand holds the mouth-piece in the correct position.

28. Foot-operated melodica

   This instrument is played by the use of the same appliances described in no. 27.

29. Mini bass or bass D

   An oblong sound box is strung with four strings, normally tuned as on the violin. This instrument can be made to order, with or without frets.

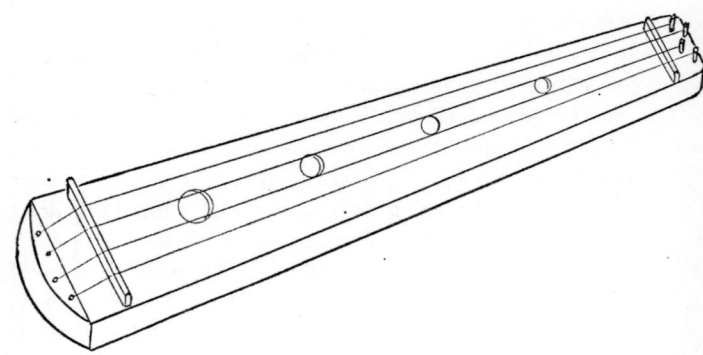

30. Electronic organ

    This can be played by a person in a wheelchair if he has normal use in his hands and arms. If the player has only one finger, an additional 'finger' can be attached to the hand, or to the performer's arm if he has no hand. A person without hands or arms can use another attachment enabling him to operate the keys by moving his feet. The organ can be adjusted to produce complete bass chords with a foot attachment; the other foot has an attachment enabling the performer to play melodies.

31. Stylophone

    This is a small battery-operated electronic organ, played by a stylus which is applied to the keyboard. The following attachments were designed to enable people suffering from a variety of physical handicaps to operate this instrument. In order to use these attachments special sockets are necessary. These can be fitted with very little difficulty by an electrician.

32. Mouth-operated stylus

    This consists of an aluminium tube with a suitable mouth grip. At the other end of the tube is a special stylus with a flexible connection, which can be plugged into the instrument. This is used in conjunction with stands that can hold the instrument in any position convenient to the player.

33. Foot-operated stylus

    The stylophone is mounted on a non-skid base placed upon the floor. The player uses an ordinary stylus with an adjustable toe grip and a considerably longer flex.

34. Hand-operated stylus

    This can, if necessary, have a special finger grip or have a 'ball topped' stylus of a suitable size. Other types of stylus handle have been designed to suit individual requirements.

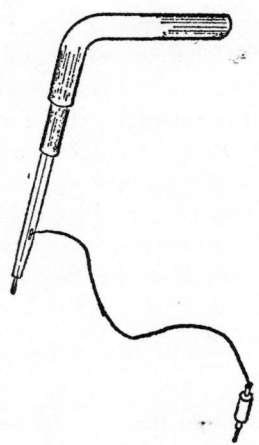

35 Head-operated stylus

    It is also possible to play the stylophone by means of a stylus designed for this purpose. The device consists of a band fastened around the child's head by means of Velcro. The stylus is attached to the headband by a tube screwed into a socket incorporated in the headband. With this gadget a small movement of the child's head enables him to play the instrument. This aid offers an alternative to the mouth stylus.

36. Thimble stylus
   This device enables anyone suffering from hand tremors to play the instrument. The aid consists of a thimble-type stylus which can be fitted on to one finger of the performer. The hand can be steadied and supported on a desk or table.

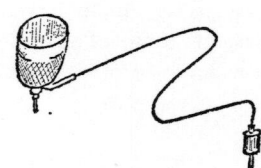

47. Arm support—for those using a finger stylus
   In very severe cases the player should sit on a chair provided with arms on which the child's forearm can rest. The limb is held in position by a wide brightly coloured band which is placed over the musician's forearm and under the arms of the chair, where it is secured by Velcro, or any other convenient type of fastening. The stylophone must, of course, be placed upon a firm, non-skid surface.

AIDS TO PLAYING MELODIC INSTRUMENTS

38. Weighted bow
   An ordinary violin bow can be weighted for use by a child who has not sufficient strength to press the bow firmly upon a psaltery or other stringed instrument. As an alternative, a short cello bow can be used.

39. Plastic bow
   A small piece of plastic material coated with resin can be used to play the psaltery if the performer has very restricted arm movement. The tone produced is reasonably good. Any type of smooth plastic may be used; a

five-inch section about a half-inch wide and one-eighth of an inch thick would be suitable, and a handle could be provided if required. Apply resin liberally to the underside of the 'bow'.

40. Mouth plectrum

    This is an ordinary plectrum attached to a round piece of wood, one-quarter of an inch in diameter. This fits into a mouth grip and enables a child without use in either arm to play a simple psaltery, or any similar instrument.

41. Plectrum with easy-grip handle

    The original was designed for a child with only two fingers and serves the same purpose as no. 40.

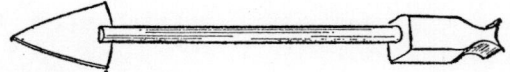

42. Extended plectrum

    This is useful for a child who experiences difficulty in using the normal type, as this kind of plectrum can be gripped more securely.

43. Plastic 'toes'

    These are attached to the child's shoes and are flexible to allow for jerky movements on the part of the child.

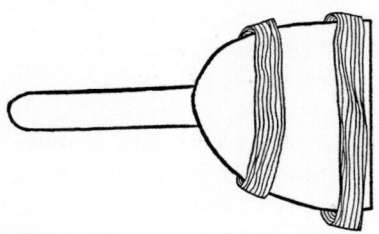

They are fitted with non-skid under-tips, and enable a child without arms to play a specially mounted clarina or melodica using his feet only.

44. Plastic 'fingers'
    A similar aid with 'fingers' is intended for children without fingers, or those without hands.
45. Holder for mouth organ
    This is a small table stand which is adjustable in height and has a spring grip which holds the harmonica firmly in position.
46. Mouth-organ holder
    For a person in a reclining position this holder can be placed on the floor, upon a bedside table, etc. and can be moved into any required position.
47. Stand for holding instruments
    This stand will hold a melodica or other instrument in its correct playing position, and enables a child with only one or two fingers on each hand to play the instrument.
48. Stand for clarina
    In the case of the Thalidomide child the clarina, a keyed wind instrument, used with a suitable stand, makes a good substitute for the recorder.
49. Music and instrument holder for blind children
    An adjustable stand which will hold various instruments and which incorporates a music holder. This enables a child to play some instruments with one hand and simultaneously to read braille music with the other.
50. For the partially sighted
    Illuminated adjustable music reading stand only requiring one copy of ordinary music.
51. Special stand
    This consists of a frame with a roller upon which is placed the music. It has strip lighting and a magnifier. The foot-controlled motor has three speeds and is capable of reversing if required. The music revolves under the magnifier at the speed desired by the performer. The player uses ordinary music, but requires two copies of each of item.

52. Stand for those with very little sight
    This is a similar gadget that will take specially enlarged music, and incorporate all the devices used in no. 51.

MECHANICAL REPRODUCTION SYSTEMS

53. Tape recorder manipulator
    This aid was designed for a person whose left arm was paralysed and who had only two fingers on the right

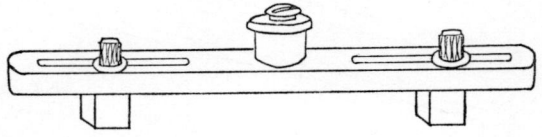

    hand. Unfortunately, the two fingers could not stretch far enough to depress both buttons simultaneously, but with this gadget the problem was solved. Its movable felt-covered parts can be adjusted to suit most makes of tape recorder, and, once fixed in the correct position for the particular make possessed by the disabled person, it can be gripped by the user's two fingers and, when placed over the appropriate buttons, a slight pressure activates the recording mechanism.

54. Mouth-operated record player
    This design enables the handicapped person to remove the records from the rack, place them on the record player and start the machine; the stop is automatic. After playing the record, the handicapped person can remove the record, turn it over and, after playing the other side of the record, remove it and replace it in its original position in the record rack.

MISCELLANEOUS

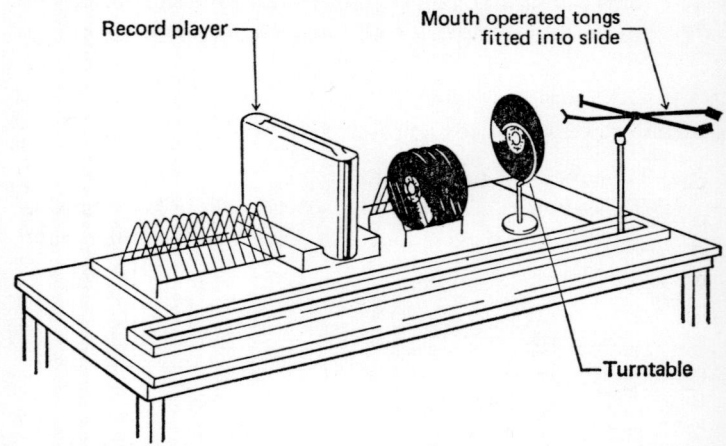

55. Magnet

This device is designed to lift rhythm cards from racks and place them on stands. The gadget consists of a length of wood $\frac{1}{4} \times 12$ inches. At one end is a mouthpiece which is gripped between the child's teeth. At the other end is a small magnet. This lifting device can be varied as required. On the top of each rhythm card is a small strip of metal. This enables the child to lift the cards by using the magnet.

Appendix B

An experiment in a Special Care Unit

When this unit opened, a friend asked if I would explore the possibility of making music with the children. They were all extremely handicapped with severe brain damage, and the majority also had considerable physical defects. They were all classed as completely ineducable, and at first sight it appeared to be a correct assessment. The officials in charge of the unit were convinced that I would be wasting my time if I attempted to teach these children, but after outlining my plans I received permission to try to make music with them.

Before finalizing my plans I spent a considerable time in studying each child very carefully and obtaining all possible information regarding their disabilities. When dealing with such severe cases I do not expect 100 per cent success, but I consider that a sub-standard result is better than no result.

Some years previously I had carried out a number of small experiments in various places, and I based my scheme on the factors that had produced the most favourable results. I had discovered that the majority of severely mentally handicapped children could learn the forenames of the other children in their group, and also that many of these children, especially the girls, had a colour sense. Whenever I assembled a number of normal girls in a room and then gave one of the mentally handicapped children a blue coat, she invariably took it to a girl wearing a blue frock. The child could not name the colour or explain why she gave it to the girl wearing the blue frock, but she instinctively realized that they were in some way associated.

I have often observed that, when painting, many really mentally handicapped children have no sense of shape or design, but frequently show great aptitude in combining a variety of colours; the resulting picture achieves its impact by the beautiful blend and variety of shades used. The results of my experiments proved that the common denominators were christian names and colours but, unlike the children described in a previous chapter, these youngsters required an extremely simple system.

In an earlier experiment I had devised a colour scheme, which made progress until I had used all my supply of pink. The new material was a deeper shade than that previously used and the children completely ignored it. To them it was not just a deeper shade of the same material, but something completely outside their experience; this time I was determined to evolve a foolproof system.

After approaching the Carnegie Trust, who expressed interest in my project and very kindly promised financial support, I visited the British Colour Council and explained my scheme. The officials were extremely interested and co-operative. The method I had planned comprised a colour scheme which included clothing, toys of many kinds, various instruments, lights, small footballs, coloured balloons, etc. I was informed that the most difficult parts of the equipment to match would be rubber and nylon. Therefore, I first purchased a quantity of nylon in a large variety of colours and shades. The next purchase was the footballs, most of which had to be painted the exact shades required. In fact, almost every other article used had to be tinted to the required shade. I used one of the paint shading machines, with very good results. My wife made all the nylon frocks. These proved very attractive to the children. Little girls and also their older sisters, however mentally handicapped they may be, are as interested in pretty frocks as the normal girl. My wife also made matching aprons for the teacher to wear when helping the children.

As all the little girls were so extremely low grade, both mentally and, in many cases, also physically, I had to commence with individual children. At first the 'lessons' were of short duration, owing to the child's inability to concentrate for more than a brief period. Each child was allocated a colour, 'red', 'blue', etc. They were quite unable to learn such terms as 'light green' and 'dark green'. The light green was always called 'green' and the dark green 'bottle'. The light and dark shades of blue were called 'blue' and 'royal' respectively.

At the start of the series of lessons a member of the staff was seconded as my 'apprentice'. She had no musical knowledge, but she was very keen and it was quite easy gradually to teach her all the music necessary for these children. She helped all the children in turn when I was unable to be present. Although I only fully describe the method used to teach one little girl, a 'blue' child, the other children only varied in the colours they used when learning. (At a later date a similar method for boys proved equally successful.)

Before commencing the 'lesson' the child's frock was removed and she was dressed in the frock appropriate to her colour. I wore an apron the same shade as her dress. From this time onwards everything used in her training was the same shade of blue. The blue girl and I played with a variety of toys. We started with simple articles such as a wooden car which we pulled around the floor and coloured balloons which we threw into the air and tried to catch as they fell, and very gradually progressed to games requiring more skill, such as attempting to knock over rows of blue skittles with a matching ball and rolling a ball through goal posts. The next step was to arrange a row consisting of a group of blue skittles, followed by a group of red ones. When she could aim at the blue skittles and ignore the red ones, other colours were gradually added. The same methods were applied in the case of the coloured goal posts. When the child could distinguish the blue skittles, etc., and avoid those of other colours, we knew she was ready to commence to learn how to play both percussion and melodic instruments. She first tapped a blue tambourine, whenever a blue light was illuminated, and later was taught how to play a blue chime bar using a blue stick. (A chime bar is similar to a single note detached from a dulcimer.) When she could strike the chime bar correctly I introduced the electric light board. (Matching the lights was a real difficulty, as the shades varied when the bulbs were illuminated, but eventually I got them all exactly right.) I used lights because I realized that a tiny baby is often attracted by lights, especially if they are in various colours. The girl's attention was drawn to the light board, and she was taught to strike her chime bar whenever the blue light bulb was illuminated. Two blue lights in succession indicated two 'dongs' on her chime bar. The other children had each been allotted a different colour and were using the same learning process.

Later a small group of children were combined. The first three children were 'green', 'blue', and 'red' respectively. Each girl struck the appropriate chime bar when her colour was illuminated; using this method they were able to play a variety of simple three-note tunes. The number of children in the group was gradually increased, thus enabling them to extend their repertoire. It was sometimes possible to teach a child six or more notes, as her ability to recognize and remember more than one colour was developed. This achievement enabled a child to play solos.

A few of the comparatively bright ones progressed to playing a melodica. This is a wind instrument with a miniature keyboard similar to that of a piano. In order to make it possible for the children to play these instruments correctly, I tinted the keys to accord with the colour system. On the child's fingers rings of different colours are placed. When she sees the red light she places the 'red ring' finger on the red note, and when the blue light is on she puts her 'blue ring' finger on the blue note, etc. This system ensures accuracy. The child is now ready to learn a number of melodies, sometimes combining with another child who may only be able to contribute an extremely simple two-note accompaniment. In order further to facilitate the manipulation of the instrument, the melodica is supported on an adjustable stand, thus leaving the child's hand free and enabling her to concentrate on the lights and the correct finger movement.

When the colour scheme was first introduced, we expected the girls to want to play with other children's toys and instruments; but, to our surprise, they completely ignored the other colours and played exclusively with their own. After the first few weeks I suggested that, instead of putting the dresses on the children, the frocks should be spread over a low form and that each child should be invited to pick out her own coloured dress. In a surprisingly short time they could do this without error, and soon these children, none of whom had previously made the slightest attempt at dressing or undressing herself, were so eager to put on their pretty coloured frocks that they tried to remove their own frocks without assistance and very soon, with a small amount of help from the staff, they were also able to put on their 'music' dresses, as they called them. This success led to efforts being made to teach them to remove their other garments, and within a few months a number of these children could completely dress and undress themselves with the minimum of assistance. The initial effort was, of course, induced by their desire to wear the nylon dresses.

When the members of staff wore overalls of the correct colour, they were asked to point to the garment and mention the shade of the material whenever a child using their colour approached. This also proved helpful in teaching the children. Later we added a very simple type of jigsaw. The first one used was a fish. This consisted of a body, head and tail. The child was asked to pick out from a number of similar pieces of various colours the head and tail matching the body of the fish, and to fit them into the correct position. Other types of simple jigsaw were gradually introduced, and the number of colours increased, as the children grew more proficient.

Appendix C

Learning games

Note

The simple melodies used in the musical games are created by the teacher in accordance with the ability of his group. They are played on chime bars or other suitable instruments.

Visual presentation helps to speed up the learning process and, if the lessons are presented as musical-games, the interest of the children, and in consequence an increase in their attempts at concentration, will considerably help in surmounting the various obstacles always encountered when teaching this type of child. When it is possible for the children to 'dress up' to represent the various characters, this enhances their pleasure.

TEACHING OF NUMBERS—ADDITION AND SUBTRACTION

The big fat Indians

Material required: 1 long low form, 2 long mats, 1 large coloured picture of an Indian. (This, of course, could be drawn on the blackboard.) Home-made Indian costumes. (These are fairly easy to improvise.)

This is a short song about the difficulty of getting a number of fat men into a small boat. The boat consists of the low form with the mats spread on either side. This precaution is taken in order to eliminate the possibility of injury when the 'Indians' fall out of the boat. The teacher sings the song and the 'Indians' perform the actions. If the remainder of the class can join in the singing, so much the better. The children are first shown a large coloured picture of an Indian; they are also shown a boat. The verses of the song refer to the attempts made by the Indians to squeeze into the little boat, and at the end of each verse one 'Indian' falls into the water. This part is thoroughly enjoyed by the children. Three children are chosen and, if possible, dressed up as Indians. One child boards the 'boat' and the teacher remarks: 'Tom is on the boat, so we have one fat Indian.' Another child then joins him and the teacher says: 'Tom and Jane are in the boat— Tom (1), Jane (2) (touching each child as she counts)—so we now have two Indians in the boat.' A third child is then helped aboard and the teacher repeats the previous remarks, adding the new child.

NOTE It was found advisable to commence with three 'Indians' and later gradually increase the numbers up to ten or more. The system of starting with a very few children, and gradually increasing the numbers participating as the children progress, should be adopted in all the games.

As the children get more proficient let them take turns counting the Indians. The teacher now sings the first verse:

> 'Three great big fat Indians
> Who were tall, dark and stout,
> Tried to squeeze into a small boat,
> And the end one fell out.' S P L A S H !

All the children shout this word as the 'Indian' falls into the water. The teacher says: 'Joyce has fallen out of the boat, so we now have only Tom and Jane. How many Indians have we now? Tom (1), Jane (2),' touching each child as before. Now resume the singing and at the end of the second verse Jane falls out and there is only one 'Indian' in the 'boat'. At the end of the third verse Tom falls out and there are no 'Indians' in the 'boat'. Other children are then chosen and the game continues until everyone has had a turn.

In the case of the really bad physically handicapped children use a mattress placed on the floor as a 'boat' and two other mattresses on either side to represent the water. The children can be lifted on to the 'boat' and later transferred into the water as required.

If the members of the group are mainly wheelchair cases, a boat drawn on the floor with white chalk is quite effective. The remainder of the floor represents water.

The bedfast children can sometimes substitute hand movements, each raising a hand or foot in turn to represent an 'Indian'. If they can each be provided with a simple Indian glove puppet the game becomes more realistic.

NOTE At first the teacher should concentrate on teaching the members of the group to notice how many children you add, e.g. 'We have four Indians, Tom (1), Joyce (2), John (3) and Doris (4). Now we see another Indian (Judy) coming to the boat, so we will have Tom (1), Joyce (2), John (3), Doris (4), and Judy makes five Indians.' Count again 1, 2, 3, 4, 5, always touching each child as you count.

When the children are reasonably sure of this method of addition, introduce subtraction, using a similar system. When Tom, the first Indian, has fallen into the water the teacher demonstrates, in the most simple language possible, the fact that whereas we had three Indians in the boat, one Indian (Tom) has fallen into the water and when you take one Indian from three Indians you have only two Indians left, and that when two Indians (Tom and Jane), have fallen into the water, you have taken two Indians from the three in the boat and have only one Indian (Joyce) left.

All the arithmetic games are presented in a similar manner.

The school bus

This is a song about the buses or ambulances which take the children to and from school.

Initially three children are chosen as 'buses' and are placed in the 'garage' (one corner of the room). The procedure is as follows:

One bus is brought into service, as teacher and children sing:

> This is a green bus (change the colour to that
> of your local buses), going to school,
> This is a green bus, going to school,
> The bell goes 'DONG',
> We move along,
> This is a green bus, going to school.

At the word DONG the child who is 'conductor' rings a small bell or hits a triangle or chime bar. It is then found that one bus is quite inadequate for the large number of children waiting, so another bus is brought into service. Therefore, we now have Tom (1), Jane (2) = two buses. In the second verse change lines one, two and five to read: 'Two big green buses' etc. Later a third bus joins those already in service and we have Tom (1), Jane (2), and Joyce (3), that is three buses on the road. (Don't forget to touch each child in turn when counting.)

The same game can be used in reverse to teach subtraction:

On the journey from the school we have three different children as buses. The three buses are waiting outside the school. The first one starts on its journey and finally goes into the garage, leaving two buses in service (Jane and Joyce). Count as before and explain that as one bus (Tom) has gone away we now have only two buses (Jane and Joyce) left, as one from three only leaves two. The second bus then moves off and journeys to the garage, etc.

NOTE On the homeward journey we sing: 'Three big green buses coming from school.'

If you have some members in wheelchairs the chairs could be buses and their occupants drivers. Bedfast children acting as conductors could ring the starting bells. Other children could be passengers and push the wheelchairs. Large toy motors, carts, or tricycles could also serve as 'buses' if required.

In the case of a group of completely bedfast children small toy buses (or, if not available, pictures of buses mounted on card) could be brought out of, or into, cardboard garages as required. In all cases try and provide peaked caps for the drivers and the usual conductors' outfits.

When some progress has been made children, possibly the bedfast ones, could take turns as inspector. His duties would include counting the passengers and buses.

Swimming

For this game you will require a large mattress or mat. This represents the 'swimming pool' into which the children dive and pretend to swim. Line up five youngsters at the side of the 'pool'. Before commencing number the children 1 to 5.

The teacher sings the verses, counting the children as she sings:

> One, two, three, four, five,
> In the pool we dive,
> One dives, two dives now,
> Splash! Splash! What a row!
> Three dives, then comes four,
> That leaves just one more,
> Here comes number five,
> What a lovely dive.
> SPLASH! SPLASH! SPLASH! SPLASH! SPLASH!

The children all shout SPLASH!

Repeat with another group of children until all have had a turn.

This game could, of course, be played when visiting a real swimming pool.

Ten little girls and boys

First arrange a row of children; nine should sit on the floor or on chairs, while the tenth child stands. When the words 'One more popped up' are sung, the child next in line stands. The children who are standing do the necessary actions where possible. The words of the song are as follows:

> One lovely little child tried hard to say 'BOO',
> One lovely little child tried hard to say 'BOO',
> One more popped up, then we had two.
>> (Count Daphne 1, Cilla 2.
>> Always count at the end of each verse, adding
>> the name of the additional child.)
>
> Two little girls and boys, good as good can be,
> One more popped up, then we had three.
>
> Three little girls and boys walked around the floor,
> One more popped up, then we had four.
>
> Four little girls and boys run round all alive,
> One more popped up, then we had five.
>
> Five little girls and boys beat their drums with sticks,
> One more popped up, then we had six.
>
> Six little girls and boys travelled down to Devon,
> One more popped up, then we had seven.
>
> Seven little girls and boys trotted home quite late,
> One more popped up, then we had eight.
>
> Eight little girls and boys had a ball of twine,
> One more popped up, then we had nine.
>
> Nine little girls and boys clapped their hands and then
> One more popped up, so we had ten.

Children in wheelchairs could be pushed, or move themselves forward, as required.

Bedfast or otherwise immobile children should raise their hands if possible; you then count hands; or each could display a small doll at the appropriate time.

Ten green bottles

For this game a long low form is required, on to which the

children step one at a time, as indicated by the words of the song.

Count the 'bottles'—Tom (1), etc.—at the beginning and end of each verse:

> One green bottle standing on the wall, (1st child stands)
> One green bottle standing on the wall,
> This green bottle stands so straight and tall,
> One green bottle standing on the wall.
> Two green bottles standing on the wall, (2nd child stands,
>   and so on up to 10)

If the children are physically unable to climb on to a form, a chalk mark can be drawn on the floor to represent the wall. The children are assisted forward as required. Wheelchair children would also require the chalk mark. In the case of the wheelchair child use the word 'sitting' or 'sits' in place of 'stands'.

It is possible for bedfast children to use plastic toy milk bottles, each holding up a bottle at the appropriate time, the teacher counting and naming the children as before.

In cases where a child is unable to move his arms but has any leg movement, he can use foot puppets.

The bedfast child sings 'lies so straight and tall'.

Musical hopping

Place a child at one end of the room and eleven other children at the opposite end. Point out that we have Miranda standing by herself. When the music starts one of the eleven children hops in time to the music until she reaches Miranda. Stop the music and say: 'Jacqueline has now come to Miranda, so we have Miranda, 1, and Jacqueline, 2 children.' Resume the music and let another child hop until she joins the other two children. We then count and find we have three girls. Continue until all have had a turn.

Although this game is not suitable for some of the physically handicapped children, it is excellent for the backward, educationally subnormal, and severely subnormal children, and also for wheelchair cases, who move forward in time to the music, and for children using walking aids.

The meadow song

Arrange a row of chairs across the room, leaving an open 'gateway' for the children to enter the 'meadow'.

The children assemble outside the 'meadow', one child entering at the beginning of each verse.

> Philip and his dog (Bow Wow)
> Go into the meadow,
> Philip and his dog (Bow Wow)
> Are inside the meadow.
> (One child is now inside the meadow)
>
> Janice and her cow (Moo Moo)
> (Now we have two children in the meadow. Philip 1, Janice 2.)
>
> Peter and his duck (Quack Quack)
>
> Shirley and her sheep (Baa Baa)
>
> Nora and her doves (Coo Coo)
>
> Susan and her cats (Me-ow Me-ow)
>
> Frankie and his donkey (Hee Haw Hee Haw)
>
> Cilla and her bird (Tweet Tweet)
>
> Cyril and his hen (Cluck Cluck)
>
> Freda and her horse (Neigh Neigh)

Ten in the bed

Material required:
A large rug or mattress placed upon the floor serves as a bed. One child lies upon it. Partially immobile children can be

lifted in the bed. If the youngsters are in wheelchairs draw a 'bed' on the floor and move the chairs on as required. Have nine other children standing by the bed.
Sing:

> There was one in the bed
> And another child said
> 'Move over, move over'.
> So the child moved over
> And another got in.
>
> There were two in the bed
> And another child said
> 'Move over, move over'.
> So they both moved over
> And another got in . . . etc.

Count the children between each verse.

Pass the parcel

This is a very elementary number game.
Materials required:
Cardboard boxes, each containing a few small articles (or perhaps sweets could be used occasionally). In the early stages it is advisable to limit the contents to not more than three articles; gradually increase the number of items as the children grow more proficient.

The children sit in a circle. Give one child a box to hold. When the music starts the child hands the parcel to the youngster on his right. This child immediately passes it on, and this continues until the music stops. The child then holding the box must open it and count the contents. If the child's answer is correct he remains in the game.

Remove the box and replace it with another which may, or may not, contain a different number of articles.

Musical clapping

Team 1

Place twelve children behind a screen. When the music starts they march around the room in single file, once only, and then disappear behind the screen. Keep repeating this procedure, changing the number of children in the file each time, e.g. first time two children, second time eight children, third time five children, fourth time six children, etc. This can be repeated as many times as required.

Team 2

Twelve members sit or stand at the end of the room. When the first group of Team 1 members appears, child No. 1 in Team 2 must count how many children are marching and then clap the appropriate number of times, e.g. if there were four children marching the child claps four times, etc. Continue until all the children have had a turn clapping, then change the teams—Team 2 march, Team 1 clap. The team with the largest number of correct clappers wins the game. Wheelchairs are no obstacle in this game, but if a child has only the use of one hand and no finger movement use Japanese castas, which can be placed on a table or on the child's lap and can be pressed with the palm of one hand. The castas, which can be obtained to order from many large music stores, have many uses in the teaching of music to the handicapped, and are quite inexpensive. Tapping instead of clapping would be possible where the child has only foot movement.

Bedfast children can participate if dolls or toy animals are placed on a trolley and wheeled to the bedside of each child in turn. (Always change the number of toys for each child.) The patient could perhaps signal with his fingers or in any other way possible. The tapping of Japanese castas, or tapping the bedrail with a stick, could provide a solution to the difficulty. If a child cannot use his hands or feet, he could use his mouth to ring a bell. He could also 'count' by opening and closing his eyes the appropriate number of times.

The ten ducks

For demonstration purposes the teacher can first sing the song using ten toy ducks and removing one at the end of each verse. Count those remaining and explain that we had ten ducks and that we have taken one away, so that when we take one duck from ten ducks only nine ducks remain. This method is particularly useful where the children are so handicapped as to be completely immobile. Where possible repeat the song using children as 'ducks'. One 'duck' swims away at the end of each verse. Start with ten ducks and continue until only one remains. Wheelchair children play just as ordinary mobile youngsters. Bedfast groups use the toy ducks, as explained above, placing them in a suitable position for visibility from all the beds simultaneously.

> Ten little ducklings swimming out to sea,
> If one swam away, how many would there be?
>
> Nine little ducklings swimming out to sea,
> If one swam away, how many would there be?
>   (and so on, down to 'one')

Do you know?

Arrange the children in a line. Commence the song. At the words 'One little girl said she had to go' one child walks away, so now we only have nine little girls, as one has been taken away from the ten girls we had at first.

Continue the song, subtracting at the end of each verse:

> Ten little girls stood in a row.
> One little girl said she had to go.
> How many were left? Do you know?

> Nine little girls stood in a row,
> One little girl said she had to go.
> How many were left? Do you know?
> (and so on, down to 'one')

The children in wheelchairs are pushed away as necessary. Bedfast children can take part if you place a small paper screen in front of each child who is supposed to have gone away. Alternatively, use dolls standing upright and place each doll flat on the child's bed when she has gone away.

Centre chair

For a group of twelve children you will require thirteen chairs, six arranged in a row on one side of the room and six on the other side. Place the thirteenth chair in the centre of the room. Divide the children into two teams and seat them on the chairs. Count the children in each team (Tom—1, etc.), then call out the first child from both teams. Place them by the centre chair and commence the music. Both children circle the chair, but as soon as the music stops each tries to be first to sit on the chair. The winner returns to his team, resuming his former seat. The loser is out of the game and sits on the floor or on a seat away from his group.

Count the children again. Say: 'Team 1 has Doreen (1), Joseph (2), Marie (3), Percy (4), Vera (5), Basil (6). Six members in the game so nobody has been taken from their group. Team 2 has Janice (1), John (2), Jennifer (3), George (4), Sandra (5). Five people in their group. One member, Cora, has been taken from the team, so as you can see if you take one child from six children you have only five children left.' Continue this until all the members of the teams have had a turn. At the end you count how many members remain on the seats; the larger number constitutes the winning team.

For wheelchair cases draw a white semicircle on the floor and then, using red chalk, draw a straight line joining the two ends of the semicircle. This is the 'garage', the red line representing the entrance. Choose two children who either wheel themselves or are pushed around the outside of the 'garage'. When the music stops the nearest child can cross the red line and enter the 'garage'. In order to prevent a possible collision between two excited children endeavouring to turn around too rapidly when the music ceases, only clockwise movement is permitted. Continue the game as suggested for mobile children.

Musical hop

Arrange twelve children in a row. Name and count them (Tom 1, etc.). When the music starts the first child hops in time with the music until she reaches the other end of the room. The teacher remarks: 'Daphne has hopped away from us, so we must count and find out how many are left.' On discovering that we have eleven children left, explain that when one child is taken away from twelve children you have only eleven remaining.

Repeat as before until eleven of the children have hopped away.

Although the game is not suitable for many of the physically handicapped children, it is excellent for the backward, educationally subnormal, and severely subnormal children.

Musical bumps

Any number of children can play, but in the following example it is assumed that twelve children are taking part in the game.

First assemble the children in a line and count them. Then start the music and play the game in the normal way, except that the last child to 'bump' when the music stops is removed to the opposite side of the room, and the teacher says: 'We had twelve children when we started this game, but now we have taken Jean away.' Point to the child as you speak. 'How many children have we left?' Count and discover that we have only eleven children left. 'So when we take one child away from twelve children only eleven children remain.' Repeat the counting before restarting the game, then resume and continue until only one child of the original twelve remains.

This game is, of course, only for educationally subnormal and severely subnormal children.

The meadow song

Arrange a row of chairs across the room, leaving an open 'gateway' for the children to make their exit from the 'meadow'.

Assemble all the children inside the 'meadow', one child leaving at the beginning of each verse:

> Philip and his dog (Bow Wow)
> Go out of the meadow.
> Philip and his dog (Bow Wow)
> Are out of the meadow.
> (Count and subtract at end of each verse.)
>
> Janice and her cow (Moo Moo)
> Go out of the meadow.
>
> Peter and his duck (Quack Quack)
>
> Shirley and her sheep (Baa Baa)
>
> Nora and her doves (Coo Coo)
>
> Susan and her cat (Me-ow Me-ow)
>
> Frankie and his donkey (Hee Haw Hee Haw)
>
> Cilla and her bird (Tweet Tweet)
>
> Cyril and his hen (Cluck Cluck)
>
> Freda and her horse (Neigh Neigh)

Ten in the bed

Material required:

A large rug or mattress placed on the floor serves as a bed. Ten children lie upon it. Partially immobile children can be lifted on and off the 'bed'. If the children are in wheelchairs draw a 'bed' on the floor and move the chairs off as required Before commencing this game count and name the children. Then sing:

> There were ten in the bed,
> And the little one said:
> 'Roll over, roll over'.
> So they all rolled over,
> And one fell out.

Then children roll over and the end child rolls off the rug and is out.

Before starting the next verse, say: 'Patricia has rolled out of bed, so there are only nine children in bed.' Continue until all the children have rolled out.

Name the rhythm

The purpose of this game is the recognition of rhythms and practice in subtraction.

Material required:

Percussion instruments if possible; if these are not available the children can clap the rhythms. Pictures of Ann (♩), Shirley (♫) and other notes.

Arrange the children in groups, with an equal number in each. The teams sit facing each other. The teacher first demonstrates 'Ann' (♩) and 'Shirley' (♫). In the early stages only use these two note values. Gradually add others as the children become more proficient. Before beginning count the children in each team. Now play either 'Ann' (♩) or 'Shirley' (♫). The first child in Team One has to say if you have played 'Ann' or 'Shirley'. If her answer is correct she remains seated; otherwise she must stand behind her chair. You count the children who are sitting and say: 'We had twelve children sitting. How many are left now Jane is standing?' Jane's team is awarded a point if they give the correct answer. Continue, testing each team alternately. When they are more proficient they can test each other, e.g. Team One may play 'Elizabeth'. Team Two must then produce her picture. They test each other alternately.

They are now ready to play and identify groups of names played in succession e.g. 'Ann, Barbara, Shirley,' 'Shirley, Elizabeth, Ann,' etc. Do not forget to count and subtract each time a child has to stand behind the chair.

Children in wheelchairs move back if they are out of the game. Bedfast children are each given a toy. If their answer is incorrect the toy is forfeited and the team with the larger number of toys is the winner.

Ten green bottles
The children stand upon a low form, stepping off one at a time, as indicated by the words of the song. The children's movements can be modified as necessary.

> Ten green bottles standing on the wall,
> Ten green bottles standing on the wall,
> If one green bottle should accidentally fall,
> That leaves nine green bottles standing on the wall.
>
> Nine green bottles standing on the wall,
>   (and so on, down to 'one')

SUBTRACTION

Ten little girls and boys
Arrange ten children standing in a row. Place mats or mattresses on the floor in front of the children. Children confined to wheelchairs are pushed forward at the appropriate time. Bedfast children could hold up dolls or use glove puppets, letting them fall as required. Children without use in either arms or legs could blow card dolls over.

Before commencing count and name each child: 'Daphne 1, Rita 2' etc. When the children sing 'one fell over', the end

They Can Make Music

child falls on to the mat; the teacher then counts the remaining children and they all discover that one child taken from ten children leaves nine children, etc.

> Ten little girls and boys going out to dine,
> Ten little girls and boys going out to dine,
> One fell over, then we had nine.
>
> Nine little girls and boys standing up so straight,
> One fell over, then we had eight.
>
> Eight little girls and boys travelled down to Devon,
> One fell over then we had seven.
>
> Seven little girls and boys did some clever tricks,
> One fell over, then we had six.
>
> Six little girls and boys in a pool did dive,
> One fell over, then we had five.
>
> Five little girls and boys knocked upon my door,
> One fell over, then we had four.
>
> Four little girls and boys had a cup of tea,
> One fell over, then we had three.
>
> Three little girls and boys were a jolly crew,
> One fell over, then we had two.
>
> Two little girls and boys, both had lots of fun,
> One fell over, then we had one.
>
> One curly headed girl (boy) was the only one,
> She (he) fell over, then there were none.

MULTIPLICATION

Pick your partner
Use all the children, if possible including those in wheelchairs.

Some of the children who use walking aids can also take part in this game.

One child stands at the far end of the room; the other children are placed at the opposite end and should face her. Play slow even chords. The child steps forward in time with the music. When she arrives opposite the row of children stop the music. The child chooses a partner. Resume the music. The two children join hands and walk back to the starting point. The teacher tells the class that Jean has chosen Miranda as her partner, so we now have two girls. Therefore, twice one makes two. When they hear the music the two girls again join hands and walk back to the row of waiting children. Jean and Miranda each pick a partner; the four girls join hands and proceed to the starting point. The teacher says that as both girls have partners we now have Jean, Patricia, Miranda and Della; four girls instead of two. So twice two makes four. Continue until you have used the maximum number of children. This game can be repeated with three girls each choosing partners, etc.

For bedfast children brightly coloured arm bands are required. The first child chooses a partner in another bed. She and her chosen partner are then given coloured arm bands to wear. The teacher says Nicola and Jeanette have both got arm bands, so twice one is two, etc. If the music is played for half a minute this gives the first child time to choose her partner.

Musical sheep

Divide the children into two groups of 'sheep'. Before starting, arrange two 'sheep' on hands and knees, one behind the other, and place another two in a similar position at the opposite end of the room. Count the first pair of sheep: 'Jack 1, Jill 2.' Then count the other sheep: 'Philip 1, Phyllis 2.' Start the music, preferably a series of rather slow chords. The two pairs of sheep slowly crawl towards each other, saying 'Baa, Baa' in time with the music.

When they meet in the centre of the room, stop the music and count the sheep. Say: 'We started with two groups each containing two sheep: Jack and Jill in one group, Philip and Phyllis in the other. Now instead of two groups of two sheep, we have one group of four sheep: Jack 1, Jill 2, Philip 3, Phyllis 4.' So twice two sheep equals four sheep. Place the four sheep at one end of the room, with four more sheep opposite. Proceed as before. The third time have eight sheep in each group. Later multiply by three and by four.

This game is also an aid to articulation, for children with speech handicaps.

Twenty in the bed
Material required:
A large rug or mattress placed upon the floor. Partially immobile children can be lifted in as required. If the children are in wheelchairs draw a 'bed' on the floor and move the chairs as required.

Before singing the first verse, put two children in the bed, and have eighteen children waiting for their turn.
Sing:

> There were two in the bed
> And two more said:
> 'Move over, move over'.
> So they both moved over
> And two more got in.

Explain that before we started to sing we had only two children (count and name them) in the bed and that as two more children got into the bed we now have twice two children and twice two equals (count) one, two, three, four children.

Continue adding two extra children in each verse.

Little girls
  1. One, two little girls—one two more;
     Count those little girls—there are four.

2. Go home little girls—you and you;
   Count those little girls—there are two.
3. See three little girls—full of tricks;
   Here come three more—that makes six.
4. Three nice girls go home for tea;
   Now they've gone away—there are three.
5. Four smart little girls come in late;
   Here come four more—that makes eight.
6. Four smart girls run off once more,
   Leaving one, two, three and four.
7. Five nice little girls in their den,
   Joined by five more—that makes ten.
8. Five nice little girls at home arrive;
   Now we're left with only five.
9. Six good little girls start to delve;
   Six more join them—that makes twelve.
10. Six forgot to bring their picks;
    Back to fetch them—that leaves six.

Have twelve children in two groups of six.

Verse 1 Bring forward two girls from the first group and two girls from the second group.

Tell the children that the first two girls have been joined by two more girls, so we now have (count and name) one, two, three, four girls. So twice two makes four.

Verse 2 'Go home little girls.' Point to two girls, who then walk away. Explain that we had four girls, but now two girls have gone home, we have only two girls with us. We have taken two from four which leaves only two.

Continue to multiply and subtract alternately.

DIVISION

Twenty-four in a bed

Material required:

Two large rugs or mattresses placed upon the floor to serve as a bed.

They Can Make Music

Before starting the song, put twenty-four children into the 'bed' and count them.

1. Sing:

> There were twenty-four in a bed
> And twelve of them said:
> 'Let's get out, let's get out';
> So twelve got out and walked away.

At the end of the verse twelve of the children get out of bed and stand in a group. Explain that as twelve of the twenty-four children have got out of bed, they are now divided into two groups of twelve children. Count both groups each time.

2.

> There were twelve in a bed
> And six of them said:
> 'Let's get out, let's get out';
> So six got out and walked away.

Tell the youngsters that if you divide twelve by two, you have two groups of children with six in each group.

3.

> There were six in a bed
> And three of them said:
> 'Let's get out, let's get out';
> So three got out and walked away.

Inform the children that six divided by two will result in two groups with three children in each group.

Other musical lesson-games can help the children to develop various basic mental and physical skills.

Musical sleigh ride

This game will help to teach the children to check the prices of goods and also to check their change when making purchases.

Material required:

A toyshop consisting of a trestle table fitted with toys, each bearing a large price tag, 1 large tray. Reins and bells for the reindeer; or, instead of having bells on the reindeer, the driver could shake a set of bells when the sleigh is in motion. Some cardboard 'money'.

The shop will require two assistants—one to check the price of the toy purchased, and the other to give customer the correct change.

Place the tray on the floor. One child, who is the 'driver', sits on the tray with his legs straight out in front of the tray. The 'reindeer' holds the driver's legs at the ankles. Before commencing the journey, the teacher tells the child to purchase a toy at a certain price, e.g. 25p, and she also gives the child a 50p piece. When the music—which could be 'Jingle bells', or any other music suitable for trotting—commences, the 'reindeer' pulls the driver and sleigh to the shop, trotting in time with the music. On arrival the driver chooses a toy and asks the first assistant the price She tells him the cost of the article and hands over the toy. The driver then gives his 50p piece to the second assistant, who should give him the correct change, which he must check before leaving the shop.

Start the music for the homeward journey. When they return to the teacher, she should check the price of the toy and also ascertain that the correct change has been given. Continue with a new driver and reindeer. On the next occasion, those who were previously drivers should become reindeer and vice versa.

Wheelchair children are already in their own sleighs. If trays are unobtainable, the drivers can sit on the floor and be dragged along on their bottoms, but first be certain that there is no risk from splinters or nails on the floor.

Musical animal spotters

This game is intended to aid articulation and also as a means of identifying a variety of animals.

They Can Make Music

Material required:
If the children are severely subnormal it is advisable to use toy animals, the larger the better; otherwise pictures of animals could be used.

Team 1 are the animals. Team 2 are the animal spotters. All the members of Team 1 are placed outside the room and each child is given a different animal to carry. As soon as the music commences the first 'animal' appears, either stepping in time to the music or crawling on hands and knees. The members of Team 2 have to discover the identity of the approaching animal and then make the appropriate noises, e.g. if the first 'animal' is a sheep, Team 2 repeat 'Baa, Baa' until the sheep has completed his journey and left the room. Continue thus until all the members of the first team have appeared. The groups then change places. The side with the greater number of correct answers is the winner.

Musical wheel-barrow

The object of this game is to aid the recognition of different kinds of flowers.

Material required. Assorted artificial flowers.

This is a race between members of two teams. One half of each team consists of 'gardeners', and the other half are 'wheel-barrows'. The children chosen to be wheel-barrows walk on their hands, the gardeners holding their legs. One gardener and one wheel-barrow from each team race together. Before starting, each gardener is given an order to collect a certain flower. You must, of course, specify two different varieties, otherwise one gardener could copy the other.

The flowers are placed on the floor or upon a low table at the opposite end of the room. Play a march. The gardeners must walk in time with the music. When the flowers are reached, they must quickly pick up the variety ordered and place it in the wheel-barrow—on the other child's back—and return to the starting point. If the flower drops off the barrow, the gardener must go back and collect another one. As they become more proficient, they could be asked to bring two or perhaps three different varieties each time.

At a later stage this game could be expanded to include numbers. The gardener should then be ordered to bring four roses or three daffodils, etc. Choose all the brighter children as gardeners and the dull ones as wheel-barrows for the first round. Then the gardeners could become wheel-barrows for the second round, thus giving all a chance of success.

NOTE: Wheelchairs could become wheel-barrows pushed by physically fit people. There could be a possibility of some of the children who use walking aids becoming wheel-barrows, but great caution must be observed when choosing these children to avoid all possibility of injury.

Birds and animals

This song is intended as an aid to articulation and is also an exercise in subtraction.

Twelve children stand or sit in a row. Before commencing, the teacher counts and names each child. She, and those children who can, sing the first line of the song. Those with speech difficulties may possibly only attempt to imitate the animals.

After singing 'One little horse said "neigh"', the first child moves forwards and repeats 'neigh'. The teacher counts the other children and explains that as Jill has gone, only eleven children remain. Continue the song, subtracting the youngsters until all the children have moved forward.

> One little horse said 'Neigh'.
> Two little cats said 'Meow, meow'.
> Three little birds said 'Tweet, tweet, tweet'.
> Four little cows said 'Moo, moo, moo, moo'.
> Five little donkeys said 'Hee haw, hee haw, hee haw, hee haw, hee haw'.

Six little dogs said 'Bow wow, bow wow, bow wow, bow wow, bow wow, bow wow'.
Seven little lambs said 'Baa, baa, baa, baa, baa, baa, baa'.
Eight little doves said 'Coo, coo, coo, coo, coo, coo, coo, coo'.
Nine little chicks said 'Cluck, cluck, cluck, cluck, cluck, cluck, cluck, cluck, cluck'.
Ten little ducks said 'Quack, quack, quack, quack, quack, quack, quack, quack, quack, quack'.
Eleven little rooks said 'Caw, caw, caw, caw, caw, caw, caw, caw, caw, caw, caw'.
Twelve little mice said 'Squeak, squeak, squeak, squeak, squeak, squeak, squeak, squeak, squeak, squeak, squeak, squeak'.

My friends' pets

This song is not only an aid to articulation, but also helps the child to pronounce correctly the names of the other members of his group. The teacher will, of course, use the names of the youngsters she is teaching. Any child having considerable difficulty in articulating clearly could at first just join in saying 'Bow wow', etc.

My friend Janet has a dog, 'Bow wow'.
My friend Margaret has a cat, 'Me-ow'.
My friend Tommy has a horse, 'Neigh neigh'.
My friend Kathleen has a duck, 'Quack quack'.
My friend Percy has a sheep, 'Baa baa'.
My friend Dorothy has a donkey, 'Hee haw'.
My friend Christopher has a bird, 'Tweet tweet'.
My friend Philip has a hen, 'Cluck cluck'.
My friend Patricia has a dove, Coo coo'.
My friend Barbara has a cow, 'Moo moo'.
My friend Michael has a mouse, 'Squeak, squeak'.
'Bow wow', 'Me-ow', 'Neigh neigh', 'Quack quack', 'Baa baa', 'Hee haw', 'Tweet tweet', 'Cluck cluck', 'Coo coo', 'Moo moo', 'Squeak squeak'.
My friends' pets.

If instruments, such as chime bars, are used to accompany

Musical chairs

A further exercise in addition and for recognition of various flowers.

Assuming that you have a group of twelve children, divide them into two teams of six, one consisting of 'tulips'; the other could be 'daffodils'. Each member of the 'tulip' team wears an artificial tulip; the other children wear daffodils. You will require twelve chairs arranged as for ordinary musical chairs. Six of the chairs have daffodils attached to them; the remainder display tulips. A child from each team stands at opposite ends. When the music commences, the two children walk around the chairs. When the music stops, the first child to sit down is the winner, providing the flower on the chair matches the one worn by the child. If a child sits on the wrong chair he is out. If a 'tulip' is the first to sit on the correct chair, you say: 'One tulip (Jean) is sitting on a chair.' Jean remains seated for the rest of the game. Resume with another two children. Assuming a tulip is again successful, you say: 'We now have two tulips (Jean and Carol) sitting on chairs.' Always touch and name the children as you count. Continue with two more children. This time we will suppose the daffodils win round three. You announce: 'We have two tulips (Jean and Carol), but only one daffodil (Martin).' Finally you count how many tulips are seated, and how many daffodils. The team with the greater number seated wins the game. Periodically substitute other flowers. The next stage is to have three, four, or more teams, each with different flowers. Do not place the flowers in a regular order. The better the mixture, the easier for the teacher to check the child's ability to identify quickly the various flowers. Bedfast or wheelchair children could count the number of seated children in each team.

Obstacle race

The object of this game is the identification of a variety of articles.

The obstacles must be made very easy for the children to negotiate and will depend entirely upon the type and extent of the children's handicaps.

One obstacle could be a rope suspended about twelve inches from the floor. Under this the competitors must crawl. They could also crawl through a large square cardboard box open at each end, ect.

Place a number of small articles such as pens, pencils, paint brushes, newspaper, writing paper, blotting paper, etc. on a table at one end of the room and put a duplicate set upon another table at the opposite end of the room.

Divide the youngsters into two teams. Number one in the first team races against number one in the second team.

Before starting each child is shown a specimen of the article he must collect from the other table and bring back to the teacher. The children only move when they hear the music. Any child actually negotiating the obstacle when the music stops is out. Continue until all members of the teams have had a turn. The team with the larger number of correct articles is the winner.

If possible, have two helpers who will follow the children along the route, helping as required at the obstacles and preventing any mishaps.

Musical snap

This is another game for identification of objects.

Each member of Team 1 represents a different object and has a picture of the article attached to his clothing, e.g. cup, plate, etc. or any other article required for teaching purposes. Members of Team 2 have duplicate pictures on their clothing. Arrange a display of the actual articles upon a table. Place the teams at opposite ends of the room. Team members should not be in the same order as their duplicates, e.g. if no. 1 in Team 1 is a cup, make no. 5 in the other team the duplicate cup.

Play a march. The two teams walk towards each other in time to the music. As they approach each other the children must find their opposite number. If child no. 3 is a plate, he takes the hand of the other 'plate' and the two children run to the table and collect the real plate, then run back and hand it to the teacher. The first pair to hand in their object are the winners.

The objects should be varied from day to day and could include toys and almost any easily portable article. This game is also useful for teaching the names of articles of clothing, e.g. 'frock', 'shoe', 'vest'.

Musical discovery

The object of this game is the identification of articles in common use.

Divide the children into two teams. Each child is given the name of the article chosen for him to identify, e.g. clock, table, lamp, etc.

Play a march; one child from each team walks around the room until the music ceases. The children must then find and touch the correct article. The last child to touch his special object is out. Continue the game until all the children have had a turn.

The team with more correct answers is the winner.

List of recommended music

When endeavouring to cater for children of all ages and with such a wide variety of handicaps, it is impossible to divide them into grades. The majority of the action songs will be suitable for the educationally subnormal children and many of the severely subnormal children; but only a limited number are possible for use by the physically handicapped children, although, if the teacher is skilful in adapting the actions to suit the members of his group, including those in wheelchairs and others using walking aids, some items which may appear impossible can be performed. When choosing songs the teacher must consider the I.Q. of the members of his class. Some items which are impossible for the severely subnormal or the educationally subnormal children will be quite suitable for use with many of the physically handicapped children. Extra care must be taken in selecting music for the mentally sick teenager as, although some of them may only be capable of tackling music normally sung by quite young children, they are not so deficient in intellect that they will fail to resent being taught music which they will class as 'kids' stuff'. In some of the recommended books of music the teacher may find a few items suitable for his juniors and others that can be offered to older children without giving offence to the members of the senior group and which can also be used for a public performance.

This advice is equally applicable to the operettas and, indeed, throughout the whole range of their musical activities.

PIANO MUSIC FOR ONE HAND

This list has been compiled for the benefit of any person who is only able to use one hand, and who desires to play the piano. The grading of all items is only approximate, as any disability in the remaining arm would naturally add to the performer's difficulty. The player's mental ability must also be considered when choosing suitable items.

The majority of the pieces listed can be played by either hand, but the fingering must be adjusted accordingly. It may also be necessary to move the piano stool to the right or left of the normal position, particularly when the piece contains very many low or high notes. Where it is impossible to play all the notes as written, play the lowest bass notes one octave higher, or substitute a different note in the harmony. This method will usually overcome the difficulty experienced by those who have a small hand. Fairly frequent use of the sustaining pedal will assist in bridging awkward gaps. It will also be necessary to play some of the chords arpeggio. Many simple tunes arranged for the recorder with a piano accompaniment are also suitable for the one-handed player, as he/she can play the recorder part on the piano eight notes higher than written, the other pianist playing the accompaniment. A large number of easy piano duets are also available, which can be adapted to make them suitable for a person who can only use one hand.

One player
Aldridge, M. and Rees, O. *The Kingly Book of Nursery Rhymes*, Books 1 and 2. Elkin.
　Grade: Easy.
　Contents: Book 1—fifteen items.
　　Book 2—thirteen items.
　It is suggested that the melodies of these well-known nursery rhymes should be sung and the bass accompaniment played by either hand.
Bach, arr. Brahms, J. *Chaconne in D minor*. British and Continental Music Agencies.
　Grade: Difficult—especially for pianists with small hands. Equally suitable for either hand.
Berens. *The Training of the Left Hand*. Peters.
　Grade: Difficult.

Equally suitable for the right hand with suitable fingering modifications.

Harris, C. *Studies for the Pianoforte* (Book V). Warren and Phillips.

Grade: Easy.

Contents: Eight varied studies.

Left-hand studies—equally suitable for right hand.

Houghton, W. E. *A Nature Dozen for Piano Solo*. Banks.

Grade: Easy.

Contents: Twelve items, mainly about animals.

Songs with one-hand accompaniment. Play the melody; then sing the songs, playing the bass accompaniment.

Johnson. *Eight Little Left Hand Pieces*. Lengnick.

Grade: Easy.

Suitable for either hand.

Johnson. *Eight Little Left Hand Studies*. Lengnick.

Grade: Easy.

Suitable for either hand.

Kohler. *School of the Left Hand*, Opus 302 (Studies and pieces). Peters.

Grade: Moderately difficult.

Contents: Twenty items, mainly études.

Last, J. *Right Hand, Left Hand*. Freeman.

Grade: Easy.

Contents: Twenty short items.

All these exercises, studies, and pieces can be played with either hand. Some items will require changes of fingering and also changes in the position of the piano stool.

Maxwell, D. *My Noah's Ark*. Banks.

Grade: Easy.

Contents: Twelve items about animals.

By omitting a very occasional note, and by playing a few bass notes an octave higher than written, it is possible to incorporate melody and accompaniment within the compass of whichever hand is available.

Pike, E. F. *The Easiest Tune Book of Negro Spirituals.* Edwin Ashdown.

Grade: Easy.

Contents: 27 Negro spirituals.

The bass (played with one hand) is entirely in the five-finger position and accompanies the sung melodies.

Reinecke. *Sonata for the Left Hand.* Peters.

Grade: Difficult—particularly for those with small hands.

This is equally suitable for the right hand.

Spencer, D. *What Fun.* Banks.

Grade: Easy.

Contents: Thirteen items suitable for young children.

This book can be used in two different ways:

1. Play the melodies, then sing them, playing the bass accompaniment with one hand.
2. Incorporate both the melody and the accompaniment. This is possible if some of the bass notes are played an octave higher than written; e.g. in no. 10, 'Swinging', if the first bass note is played an octave higher, the C and G will only be a 5th apart, and by using the sustaining pedal it is possible to play without much difficulty. Another exception is in no. 12, 'Swimming', where the melody should be sung to the bass accompaniment; even in this song both parts can be played, but this will involve almost continuous use of the sustaining pedal and arpeggio chords.

Tobin, J. R. *Round the Village Green.* Banks.

Grade: Easy.

Contents: Eleven items about a village and some of its inhabitants.

No. 1 'The Village Pond'.

Use the sustaining pedal in bars 1/2, 3/4, 5/6, 7/8, 9/10. Bars 11/22 inclusive do not require the use of the pedal, but bars 23/24 and the last four bars require the use of the sustaining pedal.

No. 2 'The Village Green'.

In bar 13 the bass G and the treble E can be played arpeggio, also in bars 17 and 19.

No. 3 'The Mill Wheel'.

Can be played as written.

No. 4 'The Village Church'.

Pedal bars 7, 8, 9. In bars 10, 11, 14, 15 use the pedal and play arpeggio where necessary. This also applies to the two final bars.

No. 5 'The Village Blacksmith'.

In bars 5 and 6 play arpeggio, also in bars 13 and 14, 21 and 22. In bar 23 the final notes in the bar will also require the same method.

No. 6 'The Village Postman'.

The final treble note (A) can be played eight notes lower.

No. 7 'The Squire'.

In bars 9/10, 11 and 12 play the bass notes one octave higher than written and omit the final bass (E) note in bar 10, also the final bass D in bar 12. In bars 17 and 18 play the first and third beats arpeggio.

No. 8 'Village Revels'.

The bass notes should be played one octave higher than written. In bar 1 substitute the bass note B for the note D as written; this also applies to bars 5 and 17. In bar 15 (last beat) and bar 16 play as written.

No. 9 'The Village Policeman'.

In the fourth beat of bar 2 play the bass A instead of the F. In bars 3 and 4 play the notes arpeggio.

No. 10 'The Village Piper'.

Bars 3/10 inclusive will require arpeggio playing and the use of the sustaining pedal. This also applies in bars 19, 20, 21 and in the final bar.

No. 11 'The Village Gossips'.

In bar 17 substitute bass A for D, and in bar 18 play bass B instead of G.

Tobin, J. R. *One Hand Pieces*. Curwen.
  Grade: Fairly easy.
  Suitable for either hand.
Wilkinson, Philip G. *Left Hand, Right Hand*. Ascherberg.
  Grade: Fairly easy.
  Contents: Three items for the left hand and three for the right hand.
Wittgenstein, P. *School for the Left Hand*. Universal Edition.
  Book I Exercises.
  Books II and III Classical and Romantic pieces.
  Grade: Very difficult.
  Contents: Book I—Exercises.
  Book II—Fourteen extracts from classical items.
  Book III—Twenty-seven classical items.
  These three volumes are of particular interest, as all the items have been arranged by a one-armed solo pianist. Careful study of the preface is recommended, and the student is strongly advised to note the useful hints contained therein. They can be played by either hand.

Two or more players
Brown, M. *Nursery Rhyme Duets*. Banks.
  Grade: Easy.
  Contents: Nine nursery rhymes.
  Either the left or the right hand can be used in the Primo part. The Secondo is intended for a two-handed performer, but could also be played by another one-handed person.

In this event a few modifications will be necessary; e.g. in no. 2 the first quaver in each bar can be omitted, and the note G in bar 6 tied to the G in bar 7, and the treble E in bar 8 if the player has a very small hand. In no. 4, 'The North Wind', most of the treble notes can be included in the bass chords without spoiling the effectiveness of the second part. In no. 7 the lower G should be played an octave higher than written. In no. 9 the quaver runs must be played, but the accompanying chords could be omitted.

Butcher, V. *Three Players at One Piano*. Hinrichsen.

Grade: Easy.

1st Player 1 hand. Play as written reading both staves. Omit lower notes in bars 23, 24, 25, and in bar 34 play the lower D one octave higher than written. This also applies to the note E in bar 35. Omit the lower chords in the final five bars.

2nd Player: Use two hands and play as written.

3rd Player: Play the notes on both staves. Omit the notes on the upper stave in bars 23, 24, 25 and also in the final five bars.

Duke, H. *Eight Carol Duets*. Freeman.

Grade: Easy.

Primo—either hand throughout, with the very occasional omissions of a lower note.

The Secondo part requires two hands.

Edginton, J. *Six Players at Two Pianos*. Hinrichsen.

Grade: Easy.

Piano 1

All three parts can be played by one-handed people without any alterations.

Piano 2

1st Player 1 hand. Can be played as written.

2nd Player 1 hand. As written, except in bar 2, where it is necessary to play E instead of G on the fourth beat; also in bar 7 omit the minim D. In bar 40 play A in second space instead of upper D, and in bar 46 play B above the bass stave in place of D on the third line.

3rd Player: Play as written, except in bar 4, where the crotchet G on the last beat is omitted.

Ewing. *Let's Change Places*. Bosworth.

Grade: Very easy—easy.

Contents: Three items.

'Silvertoes'
   All three parts are suitable for one-handed performers.
'Woodland Dreams'
   1st Player: Play as written, reading both staves.
   2nd Player: This can be played with one hand if the lowest note is omitted in bars 11 and 15.
   3rd Player: This part is suitable for one hand.
'Dance of the Clockmakers'
   1st Player: Suitable for one hand.
   2nd Player: Suitable for one hand.
   3rd Player: This part requires a two-handed player.

Gardner, G. *Six Duets—Primo either hand*. Lengnick.
   Grade: Primo—Very easy.
   Secondo—Fairly easy.
   Contents: Six nursery tunes.
   The Primo can be played with one hand.
   Secondo:
'Lavender's Blue'
   Play the first beat of bar 1 as an arpeggio, sustaining the bass G with the pedal. In bars 11/12, and 19/20, play the first bar arpeggio, using sustaining pedal.
'Bobby Shafto'
   Play as written.
'Song of May'
   In bars 11/12 and 23/24, and 31/32, play arpeggio with pedal.
'Twinkle Twinkle Little Star'
   Play the second bass minim one octave higher.
'Folk Tune'
   In bars 14 and 18 omit the bass G.
'Oh Dear, What Can the Matter Be'
   In bar 19 and bars 49/52 play arpeggio. In bar 25 play arpeggio and use the sustaining pedal to final bar.

A few suitable modifications will enable the one-handed Secondo to play almost all the items in this book successfully.

Georgii, W. *Einhändig* (Original pieces and arrangements).
P. J. Tonger Musikverlag.
  Grade: Quite difficult.
  Contests: Seventeen short works for one hand, ten items for three hands and three items for violin solo with a piano accompaniment for one hand.
  Sections 1 and 2 of this volume are for one hand only.
  Section 3 and 4 consist of items arranged as duets for a one- and a two-handed player. Section 5 consists of three items for violin with an accompaniment suitable for a one-handed player.

Handel, arr. Peters, G. *Air and Variations from Concerto Grosso, No. 12*. Augener.
  Grade: Rather difficult.
  Primo—from bars 81/92 inclusive some chords will have to be played arpeggio, assisted by the use of the sustaining pedal. In bar 93 omit the quaver on the lower stave.
  Secondo—this could be played by two other one-handed pianists.

Inghelbrecht. *La Nursery*, No. 262. Editions Salabert.
  Grade: Moderately difficult.
  Contents: Short French pieces.
  'Petit Papa'
    Primo—This is suitable for a player with one hand.
    Second—This part requires two hands.
  'Un Souris Vert'
    Primo—This can be played with one hand.
    Secondo—This part requires two hands.
  'Eglogue'
    Primo—Can be played with one hand, but omit the notes on the lower stave in bars 3, 4, 5 after letter C.
    Secondo—Two hands are required.
  'Je Suis Descendu dans mon Jardin'
    Primo—Omit notes in lower stave in bar 6. After letter C

the notes on the lower stave of bar 12 should also be omitted.

Secondo—Two hands are necessary.

'Berceuse pour une Poupée Malade'

Primo—Omit note B in bar 8 after letter A. In bar 6, after the letter B, the minim must be played arpeggio. The use of the sustaining pedal will help to bridge the gap.

Secondo—Requires two hands.

'Am Stram Gram'

Primo—In bar 5, after letter B, play the chord arpeggio and use the sustaining pedal.

Secondo—Requires two hands.

Inghelbrecht. *La Nursery*, No. 194. Editions Salabert.

Grade: Moderately difficult.

'Où vas-tu P'tite Boiteuse?'

Primo—In bar 26 omit the second quaver chord.

Secondo—Requires two hands.

'Le Petit Homme Gris'

Primo—This would require the omission of a few notes after letter B.

Second—Requires two hands.

'Ballade du Petit Jesus'

Primo—Play as written.

Secondo—Requires two hands.

'La Bergerie'

Primo—At the eighth bar after letter A, play the minim 8va and also at the eighth bar after letter D. At the thirteenth bar after letter D, omit the lower chord. In bars 14, 15, omit the notes on the lower stave. In bars 17 and 18 after letter D play the upper stave notes one octave lower.

Secondo—Requires two hands.

'Les Chevaliers du Roy'

Primo—One hand, play as written.

Secondo—Requires two hands.

'Une Poule sur un Mur'

    Primo—At the fifth and sixth bars after letter A, omit the lower B.

Secondo—Two hands are necessary.

Stocks, H. C. L. *Seventeen Duets*. Stainer and Bell.

    Grade: Secondo—Easy.

        Primo—Moderately difficult.

    Contents: An album of folk tunes.

The Secondo part is for one hand in the five-finger position throughout. The Primo can either be played by a two-handed person, or the two upper staves could be divided between two more one-handed persons; thus all the dances could be played by three one-handed people without any alterations or omissions.

Tate, P. *Fifteen Fingers*. O.U.P.

    Grade: Easy.

    Contents: Six nursery items.

Suitable for a one-handed player with a two-handed accompaniment. The beginner's part is very simple throughout. In most items the one-handed person plays the melody, except in 'Oranges and Lemons', when he or she plays the bass, and in the final item, when the bass part consists of one note only.

Either hand can be used throughout.

Tobin, J. R. *Four in Hand*. Curwen.

    Grade: Very easy.

    Contents: Fifteen folk and classical extracts.

All the items in this book were originally arranged for four players at one piano, each performer using one hand only. They can also be played as piano duets, or by two one-handed performers and one two-handed player.

SONGS

Nursery Songs of Other Lands, Anderson, Boosey and Hawkes.
Something to Sing Books 1 and 2, Brace, Cambridge U.P.

Time for Singing, Time for Singing Again, More Time for Singing, Breese, Curwen.
The Pentatonic Song Book, Brocklehurst, Schott.
The Oxford Nursery Song Book, Buck, O.U.P.
The Clarendon Song Books, O.U.P.
Bedtime Songs, Cook, Augener.
A Pre-School Music Book, Dilles, Schirmer.
My Book of Nature Songs, Gray, O.U.P.
Nine Happy Songs, Gawthorne, Curwen.
Children's Songs of France, Gray, O.U.P.
Merry Go Round, Herbert, Elkin.
Song Tree, Hitchcock, Curwen.
Things that Help Us, Hughes, Novello.
Our Friends the Animals, Hughes, Novello.
Snow White and the Seven Dwarfs, Hughes, Elkin.
Fancy Fair, Jenkyns, Novello.
Hymns for Under Sevens, Nops, Boosey and Hawkes.
The Oxford School Music Series, O.U.P.
Tunes to Read, Rainbow, O.U.P.
The Oxford School Music Books—Beginner, Reynolds; Infants, Firth and Dobbs; Junior, Fiske and Dobbs, O.U.P.
A Christmas Garland, Russell-Smith, Boosey and Hawkes.
Sing a Merry Song, Swift and Glauson, O.U.P.
Music Time, Wilson, O.U.P.
Sixty Songs for Little Children, Wishart, W.W., O.U.P.
Second Sixty Songs for Little Children, Wishart, W.W., O.U.P.
Third Sixty Songs for Little Children, Wishart, W.W., O.U.P.
Movement Through Song, Wilson, O.U.P.
  (Companion notes to the three books of *Sixty Songs for Little Children*.)

ROUNDS

Fifty Simple Rounds, Lawrence, Novello.
Graded Rounds for Recorders or Voices, Mendoza, Novello.
Sing a Round, Wilson, O.U.P.

They Can Make Music

SONGS WITH TUNED OR UNTUNED PERCUSSION
Ding Dong Bell Books 1 and 2, Adair, Novello.
Ring-a-Ding, Adair, Novello.
Jasper and Company, Adair, Boosey and Hawkes.
Seventy Simple Songs with Ostinati, Chatterley, Novello.
Make Your Own Music, MacMahon, Leeds Music.
First and Second Tunes for Recorders or Voices, Mendoza, Novello.
Let's Sing and Play Books 1, 2 and 3, Mendoza, O.U.P.
Songs to See and Sing, Mendoza, Prowse.
Play, Clap, Whistle and Sing, Mendoza, Novello.
Tops and Tails. Eight Songs with interchangeable accompaniments, Mendoza, O.U.P.
Three Times Three, Mendoza, Powis.
Thirty Folk Settings, Mendoza and Rimmer, Curwen.
Seven Simple Songs for Children, Mendoza and Rimmer, Curwen.
Toy Cupboard Songs, Rees, Novello.
Songs with Chimes Books 1 and 2, Rees, O.U.P.
Rhymes with Chimes, Rees and Mendoza, O.U.P.
Carols with Chimes, Rees and Mendoza, O.U.P.
Nansies Songs, Rose, Powis.
Out and About, Smith, Boosey and Hawkes.

GUITAR AND TUNED PERCUSSION
Sing to the Lord, Baxter, Feldman.
A Baker's Dozen (Nursery Rhymes), Clover, Feldman.
A Baker's Dozen (Traditional Tunes)
A Baker's Dozen (Great Tunes).
A Baker's Dozen (Folk Tunes).
At Your Fingertips Books 1 and 2, Norton.

SONGS WITH GUITAR ACCOMPANIMENT
Folk Songs and Guitars, Gavall, Curwen.
Nursery Songs for Guitar or Chime Bars, Gavall, O.U.P.

Sing Away, MacMahon, O.U.P.
Songs of the New World, MacMahon, McDougall.
Sociable Songs, Book 1 Sets A and B (Juniors), Mendoza and Shaw, O.U.P.
Sociable Songs, Book 2 (Seniors), Mendoza, Rimmer, and Shaw, O.U.P.
Gay Tunes for Recorders (or Voices), Sadleir, Feldman.

MUSICAL GAMES AND ACTION SONGS

Three Nursery Rhyme Stories for Movement, Anderson, Boosey and Hawkes.
Seaside Frolic, Anderson, Novello.
Twelve German Folksongs, Anderson, Novello.
Musical Ball Games, Anderson, Curwen.
A Hop, Step and a Jump, Anderson, Novello.
Twice Twelve, Anderson, Cramer.
Three Rhymes and Mimes, Anderson, Novello.
Tales of Fancy That, no. 1, 'A Day with a Difference', Arch, Keith Prowse.
Mixed Bag, Blyton, Boosey and Hawkes.
Two Action Songs, Bottrele, Augener.
Fairy Story Game Songs, Cartlidge, Novello.
Latin American Game Songs, de Cesare, Mills Music.
French Game Songs, de Cevares, Mills Music.
Physical Training Action Songs, Dainton, Paxton.
Play Games, Dyson, Augener.
Musical Mimes for Young Children, Epstein, Paxton.
Shut the Gate, Gilbert, Novello.
The Merry Band, Gilbert, Novello.
Old Joe, Gilbert, Novello.
Movement and Melody, Guale, Ashdown.
Ball Bouncing Dances, Gyford, Novello.
Dickory's Horse, Harding-Thompson, Novello.
Merrily Dance and Sing, Holt, Boosey and Hawkes.
Movement Songs for Infant Classes, Holt, Boosey and Hawkes.

People Who Help Us, Hughes, Novello.
Singing and Playing, Nordholm, Mills Music.
Children's Play Songs, Nordoff and Robbins, Theodore Presses.
Up and Down, Parr, Boosey and Hawkes.
Let's Join In, Russell-Smith, Boosey and Hawkes.
Wide Awake, Russell-Smith, Mills Music.
Three, Four, Five, de Russette, Curwen.
Fairy Story Game Songs, Sharman, Novello.
Sing a Merry Song, Swift and Clauson, O.U.P.
The Clarendon Books of Singing Games, Wiseman and Northcote, O.U.P.

OPERETTAS AND MUSICAL STORIES

Carolare, Ten Carols for Movement, Books 1 and 2, Anderson, O.U.P.
Nativity by Candlelight, Avery and Ratcliffe, Novello.
Carols for Acting, Eele and Davies, Novello.
Come to the Zoo, Herbert, Elkin.
Candy Floss, Herbert, Elkin.
Christmas Eve's Dream, Herbert, Elkin.
A Festival of Folk Carols, Mendoza and Rimmer, Novello.
A Children's Christmas Festival, Mendoza and Rimmer, O.U.P.
Christmas Day and Every Day, Parry, W. H. Chappell.
Rumpelstiltskin, Wieder, Mills Music.
The Boat Race, Dodgson.
The Magic Fruit, Lord.
Johnny and the Mohawks, Maconchy. ⎫
The Nightingale, Mathias. ⎬ Oxford Instrumental Series
The Frog Princess, Tate. ⎪
A Christmas Story, Winters. ⎪
Drake's Voyage, Winters. ⎭

Bibliography

In compiling this bibliography the author has included some volumes which will provide useful background reading for the inexperienced teacher, although a few of these books contain little or no reference to music.

Alvin, J. *Music Therapy for severely subnormal boys.* British Society for Music Therapy and Remedial Music.
Alvin, J. *Music therapy.* Baker.
Alvin, J. *Music in the wards.* British Society for Music Therapy.
Alvin, J. *Music for the handicapped child.* O.U.P.
Bentley, A. *Musical ability in children and its measurement.* Harrap.
Bentley, A. *Measures of musical ability.* (A disc recording) Harrap.
Blocksidge, K. M. *Making musical apparatus and instruments.* Nurery Schools Association.
Bowley, A. H. and Grudun, L. *The young handicapped child.* Livingstone.
British Society for Music Therapy and Remedial Music, 48 Lanchester Road, London N.6. Sets of Conference Papers.
Brocklehurst, J. B. *Music in schools.* Routledge and Kegan Paul.
Brooking, M. A musical experiment with maladjusted children. (In *Mental Health*, Vol. XVII, Autumn 1957.)
Brooking, M. Music in the training of mental defectives. (In *Mental Health*, Vol. XVII, Autumn 1957.)
Brooking, M. Music in the treatment of mental illness. (In *Mental Health*, Vol. XVII, Autumn 1957.)
Bruce, V. *Dance and dance drama in education.* Pergamon.
Bruce, V. (with Tooke, J.) *Lord of the Dance.* Pergamon.
Bruce, V. *Awakening the slower mind.* Pergamon.
Bruce, V. *Movement in silence and sound.* Bell.
Carlson, B. W. and Ginglend, D. R. *Play activities for the retarded child*: how to help him grow and learn through music, games, handicraft, and other play activities. Cassell.
Cashdan, A. The intellectual powers of subnormal children. (In *Educational Research*, Vol. IV, No. 2.. Feb. 1962.)

Bibliography

Cleugh, M. F. *Teaching the slow learners in the special school.* Methuen.

Dartington College of Arts. *Music for slow learners*: interim report on a project organized by the Standing Conference for Amateur Music

Disabled Living Foundation. *Music and the Physically Handicapped.*

Department of Education and Science. *Physical Education for the Physically Handicapped.* H.M.S.O. 1971.

Department of Education and Science. *Music in schools.* Pamphlet No. 27. H.M.S.O.

Department of Education and Science. *Physical education in the primary school.* I Moving and growing. II Planning the programme. H.M.S.O.

Dobbs, J. P. B. Music and the backward child. (In *Journal of the University of Durham Institute of Education*, January 1959.)

Dobbs, J. P. B. *The slow learner and music*: handbook for teachers. O.U.P.

Evans, K. *Creative singing.* O.U.P.

Forbes, G. *Clothing for the handicapped.* Disabled Living Foundation.

Gilbert, D. *Can I Make One* (Craft). Faber and Faber.

Ginglend, D. R. and Stiles, W. Comps. *Music activities for retarded children.* Nashville, Abingdon Press.

Goldsmith, S. *Designing for the disabled.* Royal Institute of British Architects.

Gray, V. and Percival, R. *Music, movement and mime for children.* O.U.P.

Harvey, J. *The junior speech training course through music for all grades of mentally handicapped children.* Paxton.

Howat, G. M. D. *Essays to a young teacher.* Pergamon.

Jackson, S. *Special education in England and Wales.* O.U.P.

Johnson, W. and others. *Speech handicapped school children.* Rev. ed. N.Y., Harper.

Laban, R. *Modern educational dance.* Macdonald & Evans.

Living with handicap. National Bureau for child care.

London University, Institute of Education. *Handbook for music teachers*: general editor Bernarr Rainbow. Novello. 2 vols.

Lubran, A. Music therapy and the spastic child. (In *Society for Music therapy papers*. Set III, No. 4.)

McLeish, J. and Higgs, G. *An inquiry into the musical capacities of educationally subnormal children*. Cambridge Institute of Education.

Moore, S. S. *Percussion playing*. Paxton.

Music in psychiatric treatment. Proceedings of a study day in Music Therapy held at Uffculme Clinic, Birmingham on 26 February 1966. Association of Occupational Therapists.

Nordoff, P. and Robbins, C. *Therapy in music for handicapped children*. Gollancz.

Nordoff, P. and Robbins, C. *Music therapy for handicapped children*: investigations and experiences. Rudolf Steiner Publications.

Nordoff, P. and Robbins, C. *Music therapy project*. New York, Foundation for Advancement of Arts and Letters.

Nordoff, P. and Robbins, C. *Music therapy in special education*. John Day.

Pape, M. *Growing up with music*. O.U.P.

Pritchard, D. G. *Education and the handicapped*. Routledge and Kegan Paul.

Reaks, B. Music as an aid to the teaching of other subjects in a special school. (In *Special Education*, Autumn, 1961.)

Robins, J. and Ferris. *Educational rhythmics for mentally handicapped children*: a method of practical application. Rapperswill, Switzerland, Ra-Venlar.

Robinson, Harrison, Gridley. *Physical activity in the education of slow learning children*. Arnold.

Russell, J. *Creative dance in the primary school*. Macdonald and Evans.

Schools Music Association. *Report on music in special schools*.

Segal, S. S. *No child is ineducable*. Pergamon.

Segal, S. S. *Backward children in the making*. F. Mueller Ltd.

Sheehy, E. D. *Children discover music and dance*. Holt, Rinehart & Winston.

Sheehy, E. D. *There's music in children*. Rev. and enl. ed. New York, Holt.

Smales, G. Music with physically handicapped children at the Wilton

Stuart Special School, Birmingham. (In *Society for Music therapy papers*, Set 111, No. 4.)

Society for Music Therapy and Remedial Music. *Music therapy tension and relaxation in adults and children.*

Society for Music Therapy and Remedial Music. *Remedial music in the education of the child.*

Society for Music Therapy and Remedial Music. *Music therapy in hospitals and hospital schools.*

Stebbing, L, ed. *Music and healing.* New Knowledge Books.

Stevens. *Observing children who are severely subnormal.* Arnold.

Stevens. *Educational needs of severely handicapped children.* Arnold.

Thackeray, R. M. *Playing for dance.* Novello.

Thayer, G. E. *Music in therapy.* Collier Macmillan.

Tibble, J. W. *The Study of Education.* Routledge and Kegan Paul.

Tansley, A. E. and Gulliford, R. *The education of slow learning children.* Routledge and Kegan Paul

Thomas. D. *A guide to the literature of special education.* University of Liverpool School of Education Library.

Unesco. *Music in education.* International conference on the role and place of music in the education of youth and adults, 1953.

Verboven, L. *The toy for handicapped children.* British Toy Council.

Ward, D. *Music for slow learners.* No. 8 of 'Guide Lines', series. College of Special Education.

Ward, D. *Sound approaches for slow learners.* Bedford Square Press.

Windbank, F. *Music reading for young children.*

Winters, G. *Musical instruments in the classroom.*

BOOKS ON INSTRUMENT MAKING

Blocksidge, K. M. *Making Musical Appliances and Instruments.* Nursery School Association.

Galloway. *Making Music with Children.*

Mondrell and Wood. *Make your own Musical Instruments.* Sterling Pub. Co.

Roberts, R. *Musical Instruments made to be Played.* Dryad Press.

Williams, P. *Making Musical Instruments.* Mills and Boon.

Williams, P. *Making Musical Instruments.* Universal Edition—Kalmus.

MISCELLANEOUS

Anderson, M. *Movement Contrasts*. Novello.

Anderson, M. *Rhythmic Exercises*. MacDougall.

Ash, B., Winn, A., and Hutchinson, K. *Discovering with Young Children*. Elek.

Barham Johnson. *One a Week* (52 Nursery Rhymes graded for College Students). Curwen.

Berel, M. *Bibliography on Music Therapy*. United Cerebral Palsy Asscn., New York.

Blocksidge, K. M. *How to use Melodic Percussion Instruments*. Nursery School Association. No. 74.

Greenwood. *Psaltery Book*. Brooks Studio, Bacup, Lancashire.

Haywood. *A First Book of Tunes for the Recorder*. Williams.

Kemp. *The Chordal Dulcimers*. Novello.

Schattner, Regina. *Creative Dramatics for Handicapped Children*. John Day.

Simpson. *Suite on Three Notes*. Schott.

Taylor. *Recorder Tunes for Beginners*. Curwen.

University of Leeds, Institute of Education. *Exceptional Children*.

Watson. *'Braille' Music Notation*. Novello Music Primers (No. 59) for the sighted teacher.

Westhead, G. *Music for Movement and Dancing*. Ashdown.

Wilson, M. *44 Songs for Young Children*. O.U.P.

Wortley. *How to Play the English Pipe and Tabor*. English Folk Dance and Song Society.

Useful addresses

The Three Hole Folk Pipes are obtainable from:
  The English Folk Dance and Song Society,
  Cecil Sharp House,
  Regent's Park Road,
  London N.W.1.
Pitch Pipes are obtainable from:
  Hohner's,
  11 Farringdon Street,
  London E.C.
Rota Tom Toms are obtainable from:
  The London Music Shop,
  Great Portland Street,
  London W.1.
Studio 49, Revolving Drums are obtainable from:
  Schott and Co.,
  48 Great Marlborough Street,
  London W.1.

Auto Harps
Hand Castas
Kalimbas
Stylophones
} Order through local music dealers.

For advice on Records for special purposes write to:
  The Education Officer,
  E.M.I. Records,
  20 Manchester Square,
  London W.1.
The Chordal Dulcimer
Psaltery
Bass D
Can be obtained complete, or in a 'Do-it-yourself Kit' (useful for handicapped children who cannot use tools) from:
  Mr. H. Mitchell,
  19 New Lines,
  Bacup,
  Lancashire.

Details of P.H.A.B. Clubs (Physically Handicapped and Able Bodied) from:
  The Organiser,
  The National Association of Youth Clubs,
  Devonshire House,
  30 Devonshire Street,
  London W. 1.

Large Ruled Music Staves from:
  The London Music Shop,
  Great Portland Street,
  London W.1.

For details of Tape Recorder Clubs, Recorded Music Clubs, and other information for the disabled contact:
  The Information Officer,
  The Disabled Living Foundation,
  346 Kensington High Street,
  London
  Telephone: 01 602 2491

For details of photo-enlarged Music for the Partially Sighted contact:
  The Head Mistress,
  The John Aird Special School,
  Cobbold Road,
  London W.12.